MOLEY

Marriage to an Englishman

(Stephen Drake Freer 1920–2017)

A Memoir

by FREDERICA FREER

THE CHOIR PRESS

First published in the United Kingdom in 2025 by
The Choir Press

ISBN 978-1-78963-476-1

To Zazie, Christy and my precious grandsons,
Zebedee and Orlando

Contents

Acknowledgements

Where to begin? How to thank for so much kindness and encouragement? I can only say I feel the deepest gratitude for every heartening word of support uttered by any family member or good friend over the last few years.

Our special thanks to Philippa Grey-Edwards, a dear friend and artist, for the charming portrait of Stephen that we are so delighted to have as the cover of this book.

Joan Gage, in Boston, wife of Nick Gage, the author of *Eleni*, a great American best-seller, and of several books of her own, read the draft manuscript at least twice, if not three times, and could not have been more encouraging. Ditto Julia Tugendhat who, herself, has written over fourteen books. They have both been my editors, my lifeline. Words cannot describe what a difference their suggestions and interest have made to me.

My daughter, Zazie, has spent a great deal of precious time patiently going over the draft and having many super-helpful ideas, most of which I have included. Her involvement in this little memoir has been my greatest joy.

My stepmother, Beatrice Dennis, read it all, made helpful notes in the margins, as well as very encouraging noises. Thank you, B.

Richard Beal, a near neighbour and friend, has shown endless patience, taken endless photographs. If I could think of a better word for a star, I would use it. And it was Richard's wife, Jenny, who, in the first place, suggested I write a little memoir about Stephen, of whom she was such a fan. Thank you, Jenny.

Miles Bailey of The Choir Press, publisher of this book, together with Rachel and Adrian, have shown more patience than I deserve. Ann-Marie Lowery, copy editor, has seriously impressive editing skills, for which I am hugely grateful.

Elisabeth Beverley, Jane and Lowdy Brabyn, Janet Budgen, Carrie Creswell, Merelina Finlay, the late Kate Hildyard, Robin Hildyard,

Beatrice Hodgkin, Kate Allan, Sarah Kettlewell, Sophie Megson, Polly Morgan, Staffan Müller-Wille, Colin and Jessica Russell, Louise Selby, Emma Tennant, Joy Timms and Penny Wright, amongst many friends and neighbours have asked, over time, how it was going. I never failed to find their interest both touching and heartening. The enthusiastic words of Lorna Brookes of Crumps Barn Studio Publishers meant a great deal to me, as did the constant encouragement and proficiency of Sarah Matthews, including her suggestion of the tiniest of tweaks.

Frequently, whilst writing this little memoir, I have been overwhelmed with doubts at such an attempt to portray so good and unique a man as Stephen. Those doubts will always remain with me.

Chapter 1

First Meeting

They were late for lunch. I had roasted a chicken.

'We were arguing about Oliver Cromwell and took the wrong turning,' Anne explained, cheerfully ...

(I couldn't help thinking that I would *never* argue with *anyone* about Oliver Cromwell.)

Stephen was tall with thick, untidy dark brown hair and little round spectacles. He was wearing an exceptionally long raincoat – even though it was high summer and very warm – which, I discovered later, he'd got Zacharias ('Zacs for Macs'), the men's outfitters in Oxford, to make for him so that the rain would just fall straight off the coat onto the ground. He was carrying a large box of some sort of English squashy iced raisin cake, which he offered to me with the sweetest smile.

'You must meet the Freers,' Anne Seaton had said. 'They're an extraordinary family ...'

I'd always been attracted to eccentric, clever men and had been charmed by Eton scholars before. They were, as Stephen proved to be, equally hopeless at the things I considered important all those years ago, namely, hailing waiters and hailing taxis. They were invariably shabby, shuffled and stammered, and were bemused and anguished by life, which I found irresistible, longing to hug and hold them. They had beautiful manners, were very kind, well-intentioned and had an abundance of obscure knowledge that never ceased to impress me.

It was 1973. I had rented, for the summer, a small terraced cottage on Couching Street in Watlington near Oxford. Called Porringers, it had a stable door, was painted pink and had a dear little sunny walled garden at the back, the walls of which were covered in an old Albertine rose, though, at the time, I did not know that that was what it was. I wanted to write a book. My mother offered to pay the rent, one of the too-numerous-to-mention, thoughtful, loving things she did for me throughout her life.

Stephen, Anne and I sat in the sunny walled garden, eating lunch on our laps. I kept asking Stephen if he was all right. He looked terribly uncomfortable. 'Oh, do leave him alone!' said Anne, crossly. 'He always looks like that.'

Later, I learnt that he'd never eaten lunch on his lap before, let alone in the garden.

I was so enjoying that little cottage. I thought I was in the country! I hadn't yet learnt to drive, but Watlington had all I needed: a small market town with streets of Grade II listed houses, a library and beautiful Oxfordshire countryside all around. I loved getting the local bus into Oxford, passing Garsington Manor, which seemed a small thrill and where I spotted bright red pelargoniums in terracotta pots decorating the terraces – reminding me of France – and which I have copied every summer, ever since.

I invited Julia Tugendhat,* still one of my very best friends, to come down from London to see me. She came for the day with her son, James, aged about two.

'I thought you said you were in the country?' Julia remarked, puzzled.

'Well, I thought I was.'

And, besides, Watlington was the nearest to the country I wanted to be.

---

* I first met Julia Tugendhat (née Dobson) in 1964 when I was working for *Time* magazine in New York. We were doing a cover on 'London in the Swinging Sixties' and, by some miracle, Julia, just down from Oxford, was on hand to help us with the research. She was such fun! The first thing she said to me, after I'd introduced myself to her as a fellow Brit, was 'Freddie, your mini skirt's much too long!' I felt I didn't yet know her well enough to point out that hers was much too short. The Assistant Editor, Henry Grunwald, for whom I was working, was very keen on Julia, personally supervising her extraction from a deep lift when there was the famous New York blackout in 1965. Julia went on to become a teacher, a psychotherapist, an author of a great many books, including *My Colonial Childhood in Tanganyika* (The Choir Press 2011) and the wife of the retired MP and European Commissioner, Christopher Tugendhat. She is godmother to my daughter, Zazie, and I am godmother to her son, Gus. I am hugely grateful to Julia for more than I can say.

It was such fun, using the kitchen utensils, experimenting with cooking as I'd never really done before. I remember managing to make some very delicious Hungarian cold sour cherry soup, which I've never made again – I'd bought a special cherry de-stoner gadget. Julia and I decided that that soup was far too good for us, and she took it back to London for her husband, Christopher.

Stephen came to see me again a few days later, ostensibly to collect the small notebook he had deliberately left behind. We walked around the small town … I spotted an antique shop – I don't think Stephen had ever been into an antique shop before – and bought a little china shaving mug which I have to this day. A memento of our first outing together.

At that time, Stephen was privileged to be working at the Bodleian Library with two most distinguished scholars: Dr Richard Hunt, the great medieval manuscripts expert, and Dr William Hassall, an equally learned, eccentric librarian. Stephen had recently had a breakdown, about which we never spoke but which was connected to the beautiful Anne, whom he had loved very much. Working with two such genial, generous scholars was a joy for him.

After his mother died, unexpectedly, of a heart attack whilst going to play the organ at Chastleton church, Stephen used to say that caring for his father for the last seven years of his life, when he was frail and bed-ridden – just before we met – was to him the only thing he felt he had ever achieved. I was to feel exactly the same when I cared for Stephen in his last years, forty-four years later.

Stephen invited me to stay with him at Little Compton near Moreton-in-Marsh in Gloucestershire where he had been brought up and where the Freer family had always lived. Working for many years in London, he had come home to care for his father when he became so ill.

In their older age, Stephen's parents had moved to a smaller house in the village that was called Catball (later Pilbridge). For my visit, Stephen had arranged everything so thoughtfully: lunches, cooked by his house-keeper, Mrs King, flowers in little jars, furniture gleaming … I knew I had entered a touching and rare oasis of old-fashioned kindness. We explored the countryside, had endless picnics made by Stephen himself, saw the Rollright Stones, which didn't interest me in the least, Stephen driving very slowly in his small brown Hillman Imp, the weather glorious, England at its best ... and Stephen, innocently enchanting.

When I was back in Primrose Hill, Stephen used to come and see me. I had bought a flat in Chalcot Square near Regent's Park Zoo. I could hear the roaring lions from my bed!

The first time Stephen came, his atlas was so old (1930) that Chalcot Square was called St George's Square. This meant that he couldn't find me at all. Finally, he asked someone, who pointed out that it was now called Chalcot Square but that he wouldn't be able to reach it as it was a one-way system and there were also a lot of roadworks going on, which almost proved to be true. But, with a tremendous amount of revving of the engine, and even getting entangled in the wire netting around the Square – the railings having been removed in the War – Stephen managed to park quite near my flat. Meanwhile, the revving had encouraged all the neighbours to rush to their windows.

I had expected Stephen at about four o'clock and had some tea bags ready. And was wearing my Teatime clothes.* When it came nearer to six o'clock, I changed into a Cocktail dress and thought he'd probably like some sherry; but, no, he still hadn't discovered where Chalcot Square was, so, by 8pm, I had changed yet again into sort of Evening clothes. When he finally arrived, he said he'd like a cup of tea! I remember I kept pouring more boiling water into the cup, which Stephen suggested was not a good idea. It was almost the only time he ever criticised me in forty-four years of marriage and was because he was exhausted, searching for Chalcot Square. (I still don't know how to make tea.) We then walked out to supper at Mustoe's, a fun small bistro on Regent's Park Road and which name we were to give our golden Labrador dog years later. (We once met Mr Mustoe on a visit to London and told him we'd named our dog after him; he said he was very flattered.)

Many more visits; summer turned into autumn, then winter. More walks, more restaurants, when *I* hailed the taxis and the waiters, exploring churches where, with a torch, Stephen, on behalf of the Heraldry Society, would investigate various hatchments high up on the walls, the

---

* In those days, I loved clothes. My first job had been on *Vogue* magazine, something of which I am now deeply ashamed: selling very expensive clothes to very rich women but, at the time, it seemed fun.

details of which he would then call out to me in a heraldic language that I had never heard before – and which I was supposed to quickly write down. (Stephen had, in fact, several years previously, applied to the Heraldry Society to work full time for them as a herald, but they said that, much as they would have been very glad to have him, his private income wasn't big enough.)

I wrote Stephen cool little letters, which he said later he didn't think cool at all, and, finally, he came to see me again.

Chapter 2

Engagement and Wedding

It was March. I was wearing my Evening clothes and was sitting on Stephen's lap when he proposed. I wasn't sure at first whether it really was a marriage proposal.

'Would you like to come and live in Little Compton?' he asked.

I thought quickly. *Does he want me to come and be his housekeeper or his wife?*

'Are you asking me to marry you?'

'Yes,' he said . . .

. . . and, then, to my astonishment, produced a most beautiful diamond ring. It had belonged to his grandmother, May (Mary) Freer (née Dawkins), who lived at Kitebrook House, near Moreton-in-Marsh. She had lost it and then found it again in a gardening glove; meanwhile, her husband had bought her another one, exactly the same. (Where is that second one now, I wonder?) I had always wanted a very old, very large, semi-precious stone as an engagement ring. I had definitely *not* wanted a diamond engagement ring at all but, when I saw this one, and heard from Stephen how he'd spent ages in the attic, having climbed up a ladder, ducking rafters, searching for the ring with a heavy torch, thinking to himself, 'After all this, surely she will say "Yes."' He was right – I did!

We celebrated with my good friends Elisabeth and Charles Beverley, both doctors who lived in the flat next door. Elisabeth, who has remained one of my most precious friends, was to tell me years later that I'd said, 'I've met a very clever man and I think I can make him very happy.' (I hope, in spite of many misguided efforts on my part alone, I still did manage to do that.)

Our wedding took place on 17 June 1974 in St Mark's Church, near Regent's Park Zoo. Stephen was fifty-four, I was thirty-four. I asked the retired driver of my great-uncle, Ernan Forbes Dennis, who had been a

Our wedding. St Mark's Church, Regent's Park, 17 June 1974

British Vice-Consul in Vienna and an MI6 spy, if he would very kindly take me. It was a link with Uncle Ernan, whom I had loved dearly and who had died only two years previously.

The wedding was conducted by Canon Francis Herbert, my sister's father-in-law. Frank had duties at Coventry Cathedral at the weekend, so our (very small) wedding had to be on a Monday. (The charming butcher on nearby Regent's Park Road got married on the same day – his shop was closed on Mondays. The butcher and I shared a wedding day!) My two nieces, Rebecca and Tamsin (Herbert) were bridesmaids. My much-loved mother was with us. It was a very happy occasion with just a few close friends. Afterwards, I wished it had been much bigger . . . that I'd shared such a joyful occasion with many more.

The reception was on The Barque and Bite, a barge on Regent's Park Canal that went through the Zoo. We walked back to Chalcot Square and found the little brown Hillman Imp had been decorated by neighbour and friend Marigold Dick. We drove off midst lots of clanging and noise and kind wishes to our new life together in the country . . .

Chapter 3

Becoming Moley

Pilbridge was a long, low and dark house with beamed ceilings. It had six very small bedrooms and a very long sitting room downstairs in which we had our dining table at one end, the grand piano and cosy armchairs and sofas by the log fire at the other end. There was a door out into the garden which was opened only on rare occasions in high summer. The kitchen had lots of buckets for different purposes, something I didn't understand at all so removed them all very fast. And an old stone floor and old stone sink.

Pilbridge

As I had still not yet learnt to drive, it was fortunate that groceries were delivered regularly from Horne's, owned by the family of the famous 1950s radio entertainer Kenneth Horne in Moreton-in-Marsh. The baker delivered, too, as did the butcher. When Stephen started explaining all this to me, I said, 'Just a minute! I'll get a pen!'

This was a new job. The laundry, too, was collected and returned weekly – absolutely everything went: knickers, handkerchiefs, *everything.* There was no question of a washing machine, let alone a washing line. (I've never understood the British love of washing lines. It goes with fresh air, something I also don't appreciate, the two often being mentioned at the same time. 'But, Freddie, you can *feel* the fresh air in these sheets,' says dear Sue Bowden as she shows me some laundry just removed from the washing line.)

The larder was especially enticing, with its slate slab and endless metal bins for tea, which was regularly sent down from London, as was special flour, soap … This larder was always firmly locked. I found this very annoying and got rid of the key quite quickly. Stephen's formidable mother, Mina, kept most things firmly locked, keys round her waist. I now know she was right; this way, no one helping in the house could be under any suspicion if something went missing but, at the time, I thought the keys unnecessary.

It was all the locking of the larder, pantry and other food areas that made me discover MOLES. I knew nothing about moles, of course, but, one day, I happened to read an article about them. I knew instantly that it was a description of my husband.

Pilbridge was long, low and dark, as I have said. Moles, too, live in long dark tunnels that they have dug themselves. They have an extensive tunnel system on several different levels (as we had). They like to live alone or, perhaps, in a field with others, each having their own separate tunnel. *Rather like a village*, I thought. Their eyesight is poor, though they are not completely blind; they can detect light and dark. They use different parts of their tunnel system in order to follow their hidden bits of food. I read on:

Moles are solitary creatures (apart from the breeding season). They live on insects that fall into their tunnels; they need to eat every four hours. [I could hardly believe this accurate description of my husband.] They construct special underground larders for food storage ... The mole stores the earthworms in a specially constructed burrow for later consumption. They work in 4-hour shifts ...

After absorbing all this information, which was the most perfect description of darling Stephen that I could ever have found, I didn't hesitate to call him 'Moley' for the rest of our life together.

Embroidery I made soon after our wedding

Chapter 4

Stephen's Childhood and Family

Stephen was born in Little Compton, near Moreton-in-Marsh, in 1920 to Major Reginald Charles Freer, Royal Artillery,* whose family had lived in that corner of Gloucestershire/Warwickshire for over 200 years, and to Mina Kindersley, who had been brought up at Eton where her father, Richard Kindersley, was a housemaster, having previously been a housemaster at Radley. (In 1903, there was a terrible fire in the grandfather's Eton house in which two pupils died, try, as his grandparents desperately did, to save as many boys as they could. Stephen told me that his grandfather never got over this tragic accident.)

Charlie's mother was May (Mary) Dawkins, whose family continues to live at Over Norton Park near Chipping Norton. His father was Frederic Hubert Freer, who had been brought up at Kitebrook House near Moreton-in-Marsh, which is where Charlie and his siblings were subsequently brought up.

I believe Stephen had no Scottish, Welsh or Irish ancestors. Those of whom he spoke often, and with great pride, were all English. But I very much regret that I don't have the strength to write in detail about Stephen's past family. This is a huge last-minute failing on my part, for which I am very sorry indeed. Stephen's ancestors meant so much to him, as did my father's ancestors to my father when, yet, again, I only remember the names, not much more.

---

*We still have Charlie's old saddle box on which I put a note many years ago saying "This saddle box belonged to Stephen's father, Major Reginald Charles Freer, RFA (Royal Field Artillery) when he was in the army in India in about 1912/13. He was posted to Ferozepove and Ambala. (The box holds two saddles and is metal-lined). Charlie used it to go riding, boar-hunting in the mountains, shooting and playing polo; also, shooting sheep in Kashmir."

On Stephen's mother's side there were the Framptons and Kinders-
leys. On his father's side, with the Dawkins, including James Dawkins
who, in 1751, together with Robert Wood, were to 'rescue' Palmyra, *
came the Annesleys, Duncombes (Lord Feversham), Sir Henry Clinton,
Lord Valentia, Tempests and the Tyrwhitt-Drakes. Many of their
smaller portraits are still on my sitting-room wall.

Stephen's upbringing was fearfully strict but loving. He adored being
at home with the ponies, dogs and his two brothers (Charles, the oldest
by four years, and Tom, who was two years younger than Stephen). At
nine, he was sent hundreds of miles away to the Surrey prep school
Scaitcliffe, about which he couldn't speak without crying so, after the
first time, we never spoke of it again; the beatings, the bullying. He
missed Nanny, Tom, the ponies and the dogs most dreadfully. From
Scaitcliffe he got a scholarship to Eton, where he was a King's Scholar.
(I found in his desk drawer many years later a little list that his mother
must have had framed giving the names of twenty King's Scholars
in 1933, Stephen's name at the top. When I showed it to him,
so proudly, he said, 'But what have I achieved? Number 8 [on the list] is
the Governor of the Bank of England; Number 15 is a famous author
…' and so on. That little framed list is on a bookcase beside me as I
type.)

Stephen was not unhappy at Eton; no more bullying, great kindness
and understanding from the staff. There was no comparison with the
utter despair he had felt at Scaitcliffe. Recently, I've been rereading
some of his Eton reports and there already they speak of his genius and
how he was so 'modest' and 'humble', words I found so touching and so
true. Darling Moley in a nutshell. (I remember, at a party in London,
Naomi Mitchison's son asking me, 'What's it like being married to one
of the cleverest men in England?' I *think* I replied, 'It's very nice because
he never makes me feel stupid.' But Stephen did occasionally say to me,
'Darling, it's not just that I can't hear you but rather that I'm trying to
understand what it is that you're trying to say.')

Stephen won the Newcastle Scholarship, went to Trinity, Cambridge
and from there on to Bletchley Park, where he worked in the Diplomatic
Research Section, decoding Turkish, Finnish, Italian and, eventually,

---

*Palmyra by Iain Browning. Chatto & Windus. 1979

Little Compton Manor, 1925

Major Reginald Charles Freer, RFA

Mina Freer (née Kindersley)

Stephen with his older brother, Charles

Japanese. (I have written about Stephen's work at Bletchley in Chapter 6.)

Many years later, when a young couple, Richard Elwes – mathematician son of our very good friend Colin Russell – and his charming Japanese wife, Haruka, were coming to lunch, I said to Stephen, 'Darling, you'll be able to practise your Japanese ...'

Stephen disappeared into his study, emerging later, saying, 'I can remember two words: cherry blossom and goodbye.'

Stephen's brother, Tom St Barbe Freer:

Tom, two years younger than Stephen, was the person Stephen loved above all others. I always understood this. It was from those idyllic early childhood days when their lives were so happily entwined when, together with their older brother Charles, after private tutoring during the day, evenings and weekends would be spent with ponies and dogs. Tom said Stephen was the best rider in the family, always being given any difficult horses to deal with. Country walks, making things – Tom, hugely practical; Stephen always watching in admiration – but all was to change so dramatically on being sent to Scaitcliffe when Stephen was nine and Tom, seven.

Tom shared the deep sadness and confusion as to what was happening – the canings, the beatings, the bullying. Why had they been sent so very far away, rarely to see their parents and their home? How could this have happened? Like Stephen, Tom was an Eton scholar,* and both being at Eton together, they were able to hold one another up throughout their schooldays and throughout the nervous breakdowns both were to suffer when they were grown up. There had never been any jealousy between them, only solid support and love for one another. (Charles, too, was at Eton, but was not a Scholar and, although they loved him dearly, there was never the same closeness.)

They couldn't wait to come home from school, though, on the way, their mother would make them go to tennis matches, which they hated. What they loved about living near Little Compton were things like riding long distances on their ponies, small terrier dogs following (sometimes deciding only to talk in Latin for the ride), examining wild flowers, birds, going on archaeological digs, finding fossils ... This love of the countryside remained with Tom forever. He and Stephen, even in Tom's final months in the nursing home, would spend hours discussing some new book about rare hummingbirds or a recently discovered Chinese Fuji apple.

Tom won an exhibition to Cambridge but, as WW2 had begun, decided to try to get into the army. They said he was too young, so he applied to the RAF and was accepted. The following excerpt is taken from Tom's obituary (10 September 2010) in the *Guardian*, written by his friend John Amis. (The obituary included a photograph of Stephen's very handsome brother.)

Tom was awarded the Distinguished Flying Cross. He was shot down and interned in Turkey, but escaped to Cyprus and then Egypt, where he became an instructor. He was active in the Sicily landings and the invasion of the Dodecanese islands. In September 1944 he was posted to 272 Squadron in Foggia, Italy. He was shot down attacking the Italian battleship Conte di Cavour, ending up at the PoW camp Stalag Luft III.

Tom bravely refused to pay for his name to be engraved on the Scholars' wall, saying that he'd rather spend the money on equipment for his camera.

Tom told me the story of how, on his return to England at the end of the War, he decided not to tell the family that he was coming home. To walk the four miles from Moreton-in-Marsh station to their house in Little Compton. When he arrived, they were all sitting by the fire, as usual. Not one of them moved. Only the dog, Twopenny, rushed to greet him, hugely excited. (How is it that we never spoke to Tom about the War or that PoW camp?

Tom was a *Guardian*-reading rebel in a very conservative family. I was so proud of him. And a most wonderful uncle to Zazie, taking her skiing each year to Zermatt and, together with

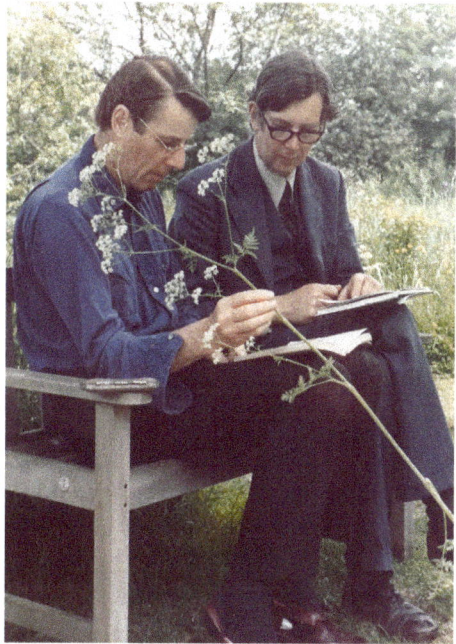

Stephen and Tom seriously discussing cow parsley, the research lasting several days

Stephen, on boating expeditions, trips to Oxford and Stratford … And we so happily saw even more of Tom when he moved to Guiting Power, a nearby Gloucestershire village.

When Tom died in 2010, aged eighty-eight, a cousin's wife, Anne Kindersley, shared her deep concern with me as to whether Stephen could cope with this loss. Somehow he did, finding comfort and solace in the Church, as always. We held a small service in our little church at Syde, beside Caudle Green, where we were now living. Our friend, the Reverend Jeremy Francis conducted the service. Stephen gave a beautiful, brief eulogy, and Zazie read out a particularly touching poem* that Tom had written about his beloved pony, Sally, a photograph of which, with Stephen riding her, allowed him, he said, to have his 'two most special people in one photograph'. The photograph, was beside Tom's bed in Hunters Care Home in Cirencester, where he died beautifully cared for by Christine Whitaker and team.

In Tom's study in Guiting Power

Tom with a blowing horn made out of cow horn

(The story goes that, at Eton, Tom and Humphrey Lyttelton, in the same class, both played the trumpet – and that Tom was considered the better player! The two stayed in touch until Humphrey's death in 2008)

PORTRAIT OF SALLY

(By Tom St Barbe Freer, aged eighty-four, convalescing in Geneva from a heart attack whilst skiing, March 2006)

'She was my friend.
Not sentimental.
But respect, you see, between two equals.

Born into the family.
Her black and white colouring like a china doll.
And her ridiculously long legs looking
insecure as she followed the mare.

She grew up brave, gentle, talkative.
Yet asking nothing for herself except that
she be not left behind.

Never had to be persuaded to do things, because
she wanted to do them.
Won all the prizes, but let me have the praise.
And did not lay me blame for my mistakes.

Six years of war, and we were together again.
But only briefly.
Now old, stiff, not eating well.
Still, however, a liking for fresh carrots.
Taking them off my hand with her soft muzzle.
Like she used to do.
Not grabbing fast, but evenly, as manners require.

It is over fifty years, yet time has
not dimmed her.
She was my friend. Star quality.
And always a generous heart.'

Stephen, aged twenty-two, on Tom's pony, Sally, 1942

Relatives: Stephen's extended family had always been important to him and to his brothers. They spoke of their relatives frequently. The one I was to get to know best, and who I especially enjoyed meeting, was Stephen's Aunt Audrey, known as Iyum, his mother's sister – and the last surviving relative of that generation. Iyum, whose first husband had been a vice-admiral, welcomed me warmly and kindly. She often shared amusing anecdotes with me, told lovingly, about the Freer family's eccentricities, which never failed to make us both laugh. We used to stay with Iyum in Devon. Her son, John Budgen, became a well-known organist and organ builder, his love of the instrument having started when turning the pages at Chastleton church for his Aunt Mina (Stephen's mother) when she was playing the organ there. We were always glad to see John's wife, Janet, and their two children, Giles and Rebecca.

Another close first cousin, who lived in Oxford, was Richard Kindersley, a wartime Russian interpreter, diplomat, lecturer and, for twenty-two years, a Fellow of St Antony's College, Oxford. His wife, Anne, was an expert on Serbia.

Stephen with Iyum, his Aunt Audrey Morten, on a visit to us, 1974

John and Jean Dawkins, parents of Sarah Kettlewell and Richard Dawkins, the biologist and author, were cousins on Stephen's father's side and lived nearby at Over Norton Park. Visiting them was always a joy; they loved Stephen dearly and were warmly welcoming to me, too. Stephen never failed to make them laugh loudly with amusing tales of their mutual cousin, Colonel Hereward Dawkins, whom Stephen had known well, John's daughter, Sarah, rapidly taking down notes as Stephen spoke.

The Dawkins' house was full of eccentric *objets*, as houses belonging to those who have lived in Africa so often are – John Dawkins had been a British colonial civil servant in Malawi in the 1940s. I have noticed, over the years, that many post-African colonials, on their return to Britain, seem unable to decide whether they are outside or inside – in spite of the cold British climate – resulting in a very relaxed way of merging the outside in, unintentionally creating odd arrangements around the house, as John Dawkins did. Maybe in colonial Africa, there were no front doors? I photographed many of John's eccentric indoor creations, putting the pictures into an album that I hope Sarah has to this day.

My Own Family: The Dennis side of my father's family came from Devonshire, described in a recent book as "an old and distinguished, although somewhat impoverished family with an estate in Bridgerule."* (One of those ancestors, the Rev Samuel Dennis, whilst Vice-Chancellor of Oxford and President of St John's College, somehow found time to be a poet, as well) The Scottish Forbes side came from Aberdeenshire and Perthshire. There were many army officers, including two Forbes generals.

My father's mother was Louise Bosanquet. (The Bosanquets were French Huguenhots who had come to England from Montpelier in 1685, many of whom became bankers.) Granny Louise's father was Theodore Bosanquet, who had worked in the Colonial Service before becoming Chief Justice of Bombay. BJT Bosanquet, father of the newsreader, Reggie, was Granny's first cousin. And it was BJT who, in 1890, invented the cricket "googly," my grandmother never failing to frequently mention how, as a young girl, she had to spend hours retrieving BJT's experimental googlies.

On my French mother's side, the family Massias were country farmers from the Charente-Maritime who eventually moved to Paris, where my mother trained as a dentist. Maria, my mother's older sister, had married, during the Second World War, Otto Polacek, who came from Prague and who was Jewish. Maria worked as a member of the French Resistance and was incarcerated in the women's concentration camp of Ravensbrück for two years. I have her *Légion d'honneur* and *Croix de Guerre*.

My parents had met in 1935 on a 'transatlantic ocean liner' (as my mother used to describe it), going from France to New York, on one of several trips made by my beautiful mother, so brave, alone, trying to escape her fearfully strict mother.

My British father, brought up in Surrey, southern Rhodesia and Vienna, worked in New York for the *New Republic*, the *New York Review of Books* and *Time* magazine. On returning to England fourteen years later,

*The Constant Liberal: *The Life and Work of Phyllis Bottome* by Pam Hirsch. Quartet Books 2010.

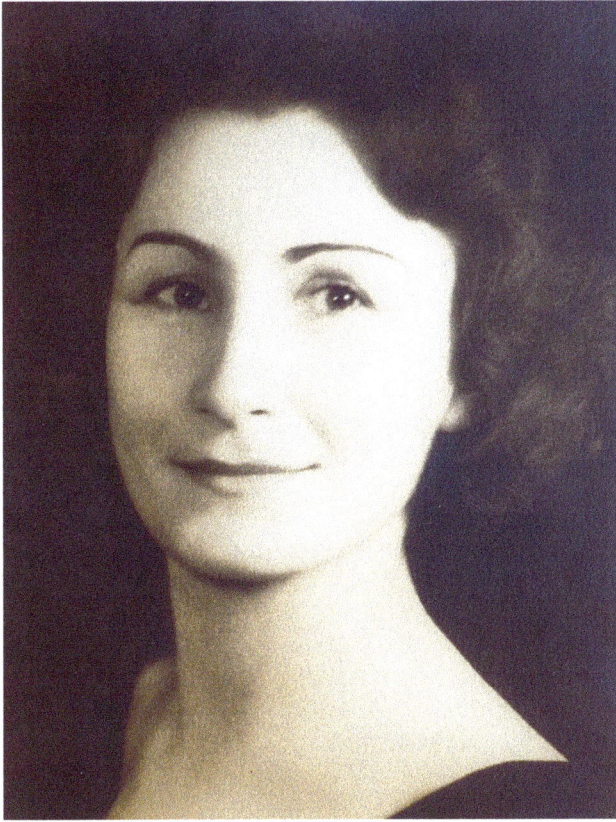

My French mother, Marie-Madeleine Dennis (née Massias). New York c. 1935

in 1949, he was for twenty years the chief book reviewer for the *Sunday Telegraph*, editor of *Encounter* magazine and a well-known novelist and playwright.

His best-known novel, *Cards of Identity*, was made into a play at the Royal Court Theatre in 1956, in which Joan Plowright, Alan Bates, Kenneth Haigh and John Osborne, amongst others, starred; there were to be two more plays (one with Rex Harrison) at the Royal Court. In 2022, some BBC Radio 3 taped interviews that Nigel had given in the 1980s, towards the end of his life, were found which, listening to in my Cotswold cottage on a dark winter's evening, were not only deeply moving but which also gave me a much greater understanding of my father's very sad African childhood – and of his epilepsy.

NIGEL DENNIS
Novelist with a satirical edge

The novelist, poet, playwright and critic Nigel Dennis died on July 19. He was 77.

Dennis had been a joint editor of *Encounter* (1967-70), an experience he said he came to detest. He would have been better known if he had published more, but he always refused to commit himself unless he felt he had something important to say. As if was, he was very highly regarded by a sizeable minority — as both novelist and playwright. *Boys and Girls Come Out to Play* (1949) won the Anglo-American novel contest (the Houghton-Miflin-Eyre and Spottiswoode Award). He won the Heinemann Award for Fiction in 1966.

Nigel Forbes Dennis was born at Bletchingley in Surrey on January 16, 1912, the son of Lieutenant-Colonel M. F. B. Dennis, DSO, and the former Louise Bosanquet. His father, who was in a Scottish regiment, died in 1918, and the family moved to what was then Southern Rhodesia; Nigel Dennis there attended the Plumtree School and was later educated in Germany. He travelled in Europe, and returned to England in the Depression.

A novel he wrote in 1930 was published during the Second World War, but every copy (to his own relief) was destroyed by a German bomb. In the early 1930s Dennis sold clothes (including silk stockings) from door to door and contributed to weekly periodicals. In 1934 he left for America where he stayed until 1949.

In New York Nigel Dennis helped translate the works of the psychoanalyst Alfred Adler, was a film censor, and became an assistant editor of the left-wing *New Republic.* In 1940 he joined *Time* and worked for this magazine until 1958 — for the period 1949-58 in the London office. He was the regular lead reviewer for the *Sunday Telegraph* for many years from 1961.

Boys and Girls Come Out to Play was a successful comic satire, but very much a precursor to Dennis's most celebrated novel, *Cards of Identity* (1955). This describes a conference of the Identity Club, whose business it is to rule the world by the manipulation of people's personalities. This was a cleverly plotted novel, again satirical of high-minded pretensions, and of people's apparent need for security at all costs.

In it Nigel Dennis revelled in deliberate "bad taste". Many critics felt that there had been no comparable satire in English literature since Wyndham Lewis's scarifying novels of the 1920s and 1930s. But it did not last well.

Nigel Dennis adapted this novel for the stage in 1956 with some success; his original play *The Making of Moo* (1958), about the "development" of a region in Africa and the setting up of a "rational religion", was also well received. Both were staged at the Royal Court during the mid 'Fifties when the reputation of that theatre was at its height.

Dennis's final novel, *A House in Order* (1966), was quite different from the earlier ones, being more serious in tone. It was influenced by Kafka. It is about a man who imprisons himself in a prison greenhouse, during a Third World War; he suffers through cowardice, but his unwilling captors — they have refused to imprison him — regard him as a resourceful spy, and he is eventually (and ironically) returned to his own land as a hero.

In 1971 Dennis published a short *Essay on Malta*, where he went to live soon after giving up the joint-editorship of *Encounter.* His one critical book, *Jonathan Swift* (1964), had been well received, and is still read. *Cards of Identity*, though temporarily in eclipse, is still regarded as, in the words of a critic, "one of the most brilliant works of post-war English fiction"

Nigel Dennis first married the former Mary-Madeleine Massias. In 1959 he married Beatrice Ann Hewart, *née* Matthew, by whom he had two daughters.

(My mother was Marie-Madeleine Massias. My sister and I are her two daughters.)

The Times, *21 July 1989*

Nigel spent his last twenty years in Malta, together with his second wife, the actress, Beatrice Matthew. He died in 1989 peacefully at our house in Little Compton, Stephen and I beside him, having much enjoyed Zazie's company, as well as that of various friends who came to visit him. There were ten long obituaries. I felt it the greatest privilege to be asked to have my father with us at the end of his life – Beatrice, in Malta, was moving house and my cousins, Merelina and Tessa, who loved Nigel dearly, were also not free to care for him that summer.

My sister, Michie Herbert, a successful sculptor, and I were born in New York. In 1946, we came to England with my mother. I was six, Michie was three. That same year, the Bosanquet family estate of Broxbournebury in Hertfordshire was sold by auction. My mother went to the sale and bought the small thatched woodman's cottage in the middle of Broxbourne Woods (Brambles Wood Cottage), knowing that my father would love it for his writing, which he did.

1946 Brambles Wood Cottage, the garden covered in cabbages, as were most gardens during the War

A great-uncle, of whom I am most particularly proud – and whom I knew well and loved dearly – was Ernan Forbes Dennis, brother of my grandfather, Lt Col. Frederic Dennis, DSO, King's Own Scottish Borderers, who was killed at the end of WWI. A diplomat, Ernan became British Vice-Consul in Vienna, working as a spy for MI6. This post enabled Ernan to forge Jewish passports, as well as being able to issue new ones. How many hundreds? Ernan, with his wife, Phyllis, was to rehabilitate many Jewish families, something that made a great impression on me. Phyllis (Bottome) was a famous, influential novelist* at that time, both of them doing all they could through worldwide lectures and travel to warn the West of Hitler and all that was to come, witnessing so much at first hand, living, as they did, in Vienna.

Together, Ernan and Phyllis rescued so many, including my father, me, and Ian Fleming – but that's another story! Phyllis had a great many obituaries and tributes when she died in 1962, including a

My great-uncle, Ernan Forbes Dennis, and his wife, the novelist Phyllis Bottome, in their London home

---

The Constant Liberal – The Life and Work of Phyllis Bottome by Pam Hirsch. Quartet Books, 2010

delightful one by Daphne du Maurier. I learnt of Phyllis's death on the radio as I was leaving for work – and heard "… the champion of the underprivileged." Ernan had only one obituary, in *The Times*, written by Frank Halliday, the Shakespeare expert and their good friend. It ended with the words, 'Friends all over the world will mourn the loss of this distinguished and generous man.' I couldn't have asked for more. Many years later, Martin Gilbert, writing his Churchill series, in which Ernan is mentioned, wrote to me saying that Ernan deserved a biography of his own. Won't someone please write this?

And it was in that small thatched woodman's cottage, with no electricity or running water, in the middle of Broxbourne Woods where, after six first somewhat glamorous years in New York, I was brought up – far, far from a village.

Chapter 5

Religion –
and what it meant to Stephen

Religion had supported Stephen throughout his breakdowns, through-out his life. It was of the utmost importance to him. He never spoke about it, never considered converting non-believers, including me. It was an example he set, without words, as well as a private lifeline and sanctuary that he valued above all else. Each night, he said his prayers, kneeling beside his bed. He did this until well into his nineties.

I respected this belief completely. I could see what it meant to him and was only too glad that he had such faith, going with him to church every Sunday with the greatest of pleasure.

I remember one Christmas staying with my sister, Michie, at Much Hadham. The roof of the local Catholic church was being repaired, and the congregation was encouraged to join the service at the main village church. As we walked towards it, Stephen began to cry. He said he had always wanted this to happen, that the two denominations be reconciled.

After Stephen was ordained as a lay reader, he was asked to give sermons at Little Compton church and, later, at Syde, which had become our local church when we moved to Caudle Green. These sermons were a great success. I'd go over them with him beforehand, fearing they might be too long or rambling, and was always astonished that each one was, without fail, precisely four minutes long. And though so learned, they were very easy to understand.

An extract from a tribute to Stephen after his death by Joy Timms for Little Compton Parish magazine, *Centrepoint*, May 2017, describes his sermons so well:

I will always remember Stephen's wonderful sermons. They were the best ever, never longer than four minutes, written on tiny bits of paper in minuscule writing. I learnt so much ecclesiastical history in those four minutes on a cold Sunday night because he made everything lucid, informative and completely spellbinding.

Chapter 6

Bletchley Park

Stephen hadn't told anyone about his work at Bletchley. He had been sworn to secrecy. It was one Sunday, when we had been married only a few months – in 1974 – that I spotted in the *Observer* a review of a book by FW Winterbotham, *The Ultra Secret*, about a place called Bletchley Park – and the extraordinary people who worked there. Stephen didn't actually approve of the Sunday papers but, nevertheless, I said to him,

'Darling, you must read this review. It will so interest you.'

Stephen took one look and said very quietly,

'That's where I worked in the War.'

I was so excited and rang his brother Tom, who said he'd always suspected Stephen had been in the secret service, and rang his Aunt Audrey (Iyum), who said the same.

Thirty-five years after the publication of *The Ultra Secret*, a charming man from the Bletchley Park Trust, Jonathan Byrne, Oral History Officer, came to interview Stephen. August, 2013. Stephen was ninety-three years old. I had warned Jonathan that Stephen didn't speak unless first spoken to and, even then, didn't ever say very much. Was this a result of working at Bletchley? I never knew. Jonathan set up a recording machine in the study and I heard Stephen ask, 'Do I understand from the highest authority that I may now speak?'

Jonathan nodded and Stephen then spoke for one whole hour without drawing breath. All those years, all those secrets . . .

'*Not* all,' he corrected me when I said this to him later that day. '*Not* all, because of our allies . . .'

Jonathan Byrne, Oral History Officer, from Bletchley Park, interviewing Stephen, August 2013

The interview, which Jonathan Byrne said would be used as a template, he thought it so good, is available on the Bletchley Park website (https://bletchleypark.org.uK/roll-of-honour/3251/). In the interview, Stephen speaks about his work in the Diplomatic Research Section – Turkish, Italian and Finnish codes – and, two years later, when the Diplomatic Section moved to London, Japanese codes, as well.*

---

* It was at Bletchley that Stephen met Sophie and Robin Waterfield (who was to become our daughter's godfather), all three working in the same Diplomatic Research Section and who would remain close friends throughout Stephen's life. Robin, whose great interest was books, had had a very varied career, including being a missionary in Persia (whilst, at the same time, acting as a second-hand book dealer!), writing *Christians in Persia* (Allen & Unwin, 1973) and publishing poetry, translations and biographies. Finally, he opened a splendid antiquarian bookshop in Oxford which was four storeys high, had sofas and newspapers and which was a huge success. Towards the end of their lives, Robin and Sophie lived in the grounds of an Oxford hospice, in two rooms, from which Robin would send regular newsletters headed 'From the Departure Lounge'. Whilst supporting patients and others, they nevertheless continued to hold their splendid literary *salons* where I remember a distinguished poet happily sitting on the floor at Robin's feet in their small crowded sitting room. His obituary. *The Independent*, February, 2009.

The website includes the two obituaries of Stephen that I am printing at the end of this memoir, as well as a charming portrait of him painted in 1944 (*Portrait of a Scholar*) by Sir Robin Darwin, Rector of the Royal College of Art, with whom Stephen shared a house in Cheyne Walk in Chelsea during the War, together with fifteen other lodgers, including James Lees-Milne. (Darwin offered Stephen the portrait for £42, but Stephen thought that far too much! I have tried to find the original, greatly helped by the very kind curator of the RCA, but we cannot trace it.)

Portrait of a Scholar by Sir Robin Darwin, RRCA, 1944

There were many Bletchley stories, including the well-known one about Alan Turing tying his tin mug to a radiator so that no one else could use it. (On a tour of Bletchley in 2009, I saw the tin mug right there) William (Bill) Tutte was the person Stephen thought the most brilliant.* Rounders was always played and must have been a great pleasure, being in the garden rather than in one of the Huts. (Stephen actually wasn't in a Hut; he was in the house itself.)

A few years before he died, Stephen and I watched the film *The Imitation Game*. Throughout, Stephen kept saying, 'It wasn't like that at all.' He had greatly admired Alastair Denniston, one of the founding fathers of Bletchley and Head of the Codebreakers, who had interviewed Stephen, and who took him on. Stephen felt that Alastair was very unfairly portrayed in the film.

Bletchley Park badge sent to past decoders by Gordon Brown in 2009

---

*The tutor at Cambridge of both Bill Tutte and Stephen was Patrick Duff, and it was Patrick who encouraged Bill Tatte to be a mathematician.

Post-Bletchley: After Bletchley, Stephen had a serious breakdown lasting two years during which, I was told, he never spoke. Not a word. Maybe, not being allowed to discuss his Bletchley work had such an effect on him?* Letters from his mother to the hospital in Chipping Norton where he stayed for those two years are so touching, from a world where you withheld so much feeling and emotion, as her dear husband, Stephen's father, Reginald Charles, had to do when, firstly, his father, Hubert, died suddenly and, a month later, his mother, Stephen's grandmother, May (Mary) Freer (née Dawkins), committed suicide, leaving three small children orphaned. May was simply never mentioned again.

When the three brothers gave me the desk of their father, Charlie, soon after Stephen and I were married, I found the bottom drawer full of photographs of Charlie's parents, Hubert and May, as well as pictures of the rest of the family, their home (Kitebrook House, near Moreton-in-Marsh), the gardens ... I showed the photographs to Stephen. None of the brothers had ever looked in their father's desk before; had never seen these photographs. I tried to explain to those three brothers how desperate May must have been to do such a thing. She and her husband had been together on a boat going out to the family's sugar plantation in Jamaica. (May wrote a most loving letter to her three children just before she and Hubert boarded the ship. It ended with the words, 'So much love to my darlings'.) On the way, Hubert suddenly died from dysentery. May, pregnant with a fourth child, had to return to England alone, bringing her husband's body home. Whilst on the boat, she jumped into the sea.

Charles, Stephen's older brother, a clergyman, said, 'It was the most wicked thing to do.'**

---

* I've just noticed on the Bletchley Park Wikipedia page the following paragraph: 'All staff signed the official Secrets Act (1939) and a 1942 security warning emphasised the importance of discretion even within Bletchley itself: "Do not talk at meals. Do not talk in the transport. Do not talk travelling. Do not talk in the billet. Do not talk by your own fireside. Be careful even in your Hut ..."'

**Charles himself was to commit suicide ten years later. The funeral was at Chastleton. I remember Zazie, aged five, taking Tom's hand and holding it firmly all the way to the grave.

I was so shocked at such ignorance about suicide – so normal in those days, I know – that I defiantly put up several framed photographs of May on the grand piano and a lovely oil portrait of her kindly given to us by Jean Dawkins that I hung above Stephen's desk. I did not want that grieving, deeply saddened, disturbed, caring, pregnant wife and most loving mother to be forgotten.

Hubert and May Freer's headstone at Chastleton

Once recovered from that breakdown, Stephen started working for the Historical Manuscripts Commission in London. This was a perfect job for him, entailing visits to large country houses, including Holkham Hall, in which he was asked to explore attic treasures and archives and where the families involved much enjoyed his company and knowledge, often inviting him to stay for several days.

Chapter 7

Village Life

When we married in 1974, I was thirty-four years old and Stephen was fifty-four. I had never lived in a village before. Everyone was so kind and welcoming. *This is going to be wonderful,* I thought. We had a housekeeper and two cleaners, one for upstairs and one for downstairs.

'Darling, I don't need all this help, you know,' I said to my husband. 'I can do everything myself.'

Such fun: housekeeping, cooking, gardening. All so new!

It was June. The garden was ravishing. Amongst our wedding presents was a camellia. I gave it proudly to Norman, our gardener, to plant. It soon died. The soil was all wrong. Norman used to spend a lot of time rolling cigarettes in a shed. He had a very bad limp from Burma. When we decided that it would be 'such fun' to do the two-acre garden ourselves, we greatly reduced Norman's hours. It only took about four weeks for the garden to be startlingly covered in overgrowth and weeds.

'I can't understand it,' I kept saying. 'Norman never did anything very much.'

This was the sort of error of judgement I made frequently in those early years of marriage. Another was to assume that all those in the big houses were 'bad' and those in the tiny cottages were 'good'. Incredible! Gradually, however, I couldn't help noticing that it was the people from the big houses who did most of the church flowers, chaired endless committee meetings, fund-raised, were school governors, opened their gardens for village fêtes, and so on. I was very disappointed. This was not at all how I had imagined it would be.

But I can now see that it was difficult for our neighbours to understand this much younger wife from London, born in New York, who Stephen had brought home. She didn't hunt, shoot or fish, go to balls, had always worked in publishing but never had a real career, was half-French (i.e. rather *foreign*), her father was a *writer*. I remember one neighbour, having made an excuse to come and see me about something unimportant, standing in my study, saying, whilst looking at me, his brow furrowed, lost for words, 'You're very *artistic*, aren't you?'

That seemed to solve the problem for him and gave me a label, though very undeserved, that I was only too happy to accept.

A Village Rescue: My Little Compton village rescue came from a wonderfully kind elderly neighbour, Marjory Nutter, who became a Best Friend – and a lifeline. Marjory took me in hand, offering suggestions and advice as to how I ought to behave in a village, saying, for a start, when making a Red Cross collection, don't leave out anyone you think is very old or very poor, something I had just done having been asked to make a collection by the vicar's wife.

'But Tom Jennings *is* so poor,' I wailed. 'I couldn't possibly ask him for money.'

'Oh, but, Freddie, he's so generous and besides he'd have so enjoyed talking to you.'

That little lesson learnt, Marjory also pointed out that if someone came to me collecting for some charity, I was not to turn out my entire jewellery box and offer many of its contents, as I had just done.

'No, Freddie. There will be other collections throughout the year. You just offer *one* thing at a time.' A revelation!

Also, if at a party you've enjoyed meeting some charming neighbours, don't say, as you are leaving (as she heard me say), 'I expect I'll see you at the Locker-Lampsons' on Sunday,' because they might not have been invited. Another revelation!

And we'd be asked to bridge parties, though, of course, I had no idea how to play bridge. But I remember one kind hostess, who very much wanted Stephen to be with them, suggesting I might sit in the room, in the corner, and read a glossy magazine. I thought this a most excellent idea. We would first have a particularly delicious dinner and then I could escape the actual bridge-playing by sitting comfortably beside the fire, deep in *Vogue* or *House & Garden*. One could hardly have asked for more.

I was invited to join the WI where I was immediately won over by the kindness of the members. Soon to become the secretary, when I met any members on Moreton-in-Marsh High Street, and they would ask me what the next meeting was about, I would say, vaguely, never interested in the talk, 'Does it matter? The meetings are such fun, aren't they? It's so lovely all just being together.' (The letters I had from WI friends when our daughter, Zazie, was born are amongst those I treasure most.)

Stephen, too, became a sort of honorary member of our local WI branch as it was so important to have someone to eat that first slice of cake. They loved him dearly.

One of the many WI outings Stephen came on was to Chastleton House on a hot summer's day. As we arrived, the elderly owner, Alan Clutton-Brock, who knew Stephen well, was sitting in a deckchair in the drive wearing an old straw hat, the middle bit missing – only the outer edges were giving him any protection from the sun – and reading a James Bond thriller. Horrified at seeing Stephen, he said to me, '*Please* don't tell Stephen what I'm reading,' and hid the book under a newspaper on the ground beside him.

Mentioning the WI reminds me of Kittie Lardner, a splendid elderly spinster who adored Stephen and who used to come and see us when she wasn't gardening in her pretty cottage at the other end of the village. Kittie, who was very thin indeed, had white hair piled up in a sort of *chignon* and, when dressed up, wore pearl earrings, a pearl necklace and a lacy white blouse. And one thing Kittie never failed to mention was the Queen. She would invariably say to Stephen, as they walked together around the garden, 'I wonder what our dear Queen is doing today?'

And it was Kittie who taught me to be punctual. Or, not to be inconsiderately late. The WI had arranged an outing and were kindly going to come in the coach to pick me up. The doorbell rang and there was Kittie. After welcoming her, I said, 'I'll just go and quickly powder my nose,' or some such.

'No, Frederica,' said Kittie, frighteningly serious. 'You are keeping all the members in the coach waiting.'

Amazingly, I had never considered how rude and selfish my unpunctuality actually was, and how it must have frequently caused such inconvenience and annoyance. I was appalled when it was made so clear to me that I was keeping a coach full of people waiting – and I have never been thoughtlessly late since.

Church: I had only ever been to services at my convent school – not the same as going with your parents to church on Sundays. I especially loved Evensong and, when Stephen was taking the service, I used to sit in the back row next to a marvellous retired farm worker called Bill Godson (on whose other side was a woman who, some would say darkly, he called his 'cousin'), feeling sure that if I listened to him singing so energetically, I should soon learn all those tunes myself – and I did. (In my will, I asked that Bill Godson choose the hymns for my funeral but, alas, his own has already taken place.)

But we were always late for the service. It was my fault entirely. (I hadn't yet had my lightning moment from Kittie Lardner.) Stephen's clergyman brother, Charles, would be waiting for us, looking angry.

'Our parents were never late for church. They were the most respected couple in the three counties,' he intoned. Terrifying. *Three* counties? Which could they possibly be?

Breakfasts: Stephen brought me the most delicious scrambled egg breakfasts in bed every single morning throughout our married life – forty-four years – until he was bedridden. It was a most fearfully serious, single-minded undertaking whilst still in his dressing gown, entailing anxiously circumnavigating the kitchen – from stove to hot plate to tray – so much to consider, his brow furrowed, the toast toasted, the eggs scrambled so that they were just right, neither overcooked nor too runny, the teapot filled and then the immense triumph of carrying it to me all the way upstairs. I so appreciated it.

Drains: Stephen loved drains. In another life, he'd have been a plumber. When work was being done on our bathroom sink one day, Stephen stood over the plumber, who was working away. The next day, the poor man mentioned his discomfort at Stephen's close proximity. I had to explain that Stephen adored drains and was truly fascinated by all the man was doing, not watching in a critical way but really interested and wanting to learn.

Summer soon became autumn, then winter. Dark at 2.30pm. No street lights. My makeup froze on the dressing table. I complained to Elizabeth, the vicar's wife, that all the leaves had gone. 'But, Freddie, you can now see the shape of the trees.' I didn't want to see the shape of the trees! When we walked our first dog, a very large, completely out-of-control male golden Labrador called Mustoe, we didn't see a soul. The village roads were deserted. Where had everyone gone?

'Darling, I can't possibly spend another winter in the country,' I said to my poor husband. 'We'll have to go to London.'

'But we can't go away in the hunting season,' he pleaded. What a silly thing to say! What could he mean?

The years passed. The garden and orchard took up a lot of our time. I especially loved the orchard, wild with cow parsley in spring and, in summer, the vicar's charming, *very* long-haired hippy son mowing wiggly paths through the tall grass to the stream at the bottom.

'You just walk through it, Freddie, and I'll follow you with the mower.'

I cut down any old trees that weren't upright. (I mean, in London or Manhattan, you didn't see crooked old trees lying on their sides, did you?) Hidcote – and Kiftsgate – masterminded by the indomitable owner, Diany Binny, who sat at a table in the front drive and who always applauded what one had bought. 'You've chosen quite the best *Rugosa* rose!'* – were our 'special places' for anniversaries and hot, summer days, from which we drew inspiration as to what plants to grow in the May and August flowering gaps.

---

*It was at both Hidcote and Kiftsgate in summer that we were able to enjoy old French shrub roses – a new passion for me – with enchanting names such *as Gloire de Dijon, Reine des Violettes, Rêve d'Or, Souvenir de la Malmaison, Boule de Neige, Chapeau de Napoléon, Cardinal Richelieu* and one that, alas, I dare not print in its original French but which the British have translated, very loosely indeed, as Maiden's Blush.

And an old China rose, '*Mutabilis*', that Elisabeth Beverley gave me is my *pièce de résistance*. No one is allowed to leave my small cottage garden without admiring it. Ultimately, a very large shrub indeed, it flowers continuously from early summer until autumn, has wide single petals starting as orange buds, turning to cream and, finally, ageing to a very bright shocking pink. A kaleidoscope of colour all summer!

Eating out was a nightmare. I'd come from a world of restaurants and pubs, all unknown to Stephen. I asked around locally where a good pub might be and off we went. But Stephen didn't know how to order; didn't understand the bar. It was hopeless. Also, he didn't speak to me. I'd sit there saying, 'Darling, *please* talk to me,' but, no, he couldn't. He just wanted to eat. We never went to a pub again.

And restaurants weren't much better. Firstly, as I've said, he couldn't hail a waiter and, secondly, he didn't speak when he was eating. This was embarrassing at lunch or supper parties. I'd always have to warn our hostess, 'We'd love to come. Thank you so much for asking us, but I do hope you know that Stephen doesn't say anything until he's had two helpings.'

This all stemmed from school where, if you were very quick – and didn't talk because you were eating food so fast – you might be lucky enough to have a second helping. It was interesting to see that, without fail, after he'd been offered a second helping by our kind hostess, he would suddenly lift his head up and join in the conversation perfectly intelligently as though he'd been listening all the time and longing to contribute. (In the car on the way to any dinner party, I'd have said to him, 'Darling, you will talk to the person on your left and on your right, won't you?' which always made him frown. He was hungry and was, after all, surely, going out to *eat.*)

As Stephen was quite a messy eater, I found an advertisement in *The Oldie* magazine for a chain with two clips that you hung around your neck, attaching a napkin or tea towel to the clips. It was a huge success and all our friends wanted one, too. I wrote to the supplier, someone called Mr Brown:

Dear Mr Brown,

We are thrilled with the napkin chain. It is a great success. Thank you so much.
And I've been thinking that if you made your advertisement a little bigger, and reworded it slightly, you could really make a lot of money. (This is only a suggestion, of course.)

Yours sincerely,
Frederica Freer

I received the following reply:

Dear Mrs Freer,
Thank you for your letter. I am glad you received the napkin chain safely.
My wife and I retired to Frinton-on-Sea ten years ago and enjoy living here, together with our dog. We don't want to make lots of money.

Yours sincerely,
David Brown

Eating in wasn't much better. I remember early on in our marriage, Alan and Barbara Clutton-Brock from Chastleton coming to supper. Sadly, we must have forgotten to offer any wine. I always left the wine-pouring to Stephen – a great mistake. I never learnt. He invariably forgot. His parents really disapproved of alcohol; their meals were served only with water. Stephen's Aunt Audrey (Iyum) told me that when she and her husband came to stay, they always brought with them a bottle of gin that they kept hidden in their bedroom cupboard.

The morning after that supper, I heard from the owners of the pub near our house that the Clutton-Brocks had sneaked out between courses, begging the pub for a quick glass or two of wine! I remember on another occasion a guest saying, longingly, towards the end of a meal, the wine bottle full, standing proudly untouched in its silver holder, could he possibly have just *a little* wine to go with the cheese . . .

Turkish Coffee: Stephen might have forgotten to offer wine at dinner parties but there was always *Turkish coffee!* Producing Turkish coffee, triumphantly, at the end of meals, was the party trick that Stephen most enjoyed and one that never failed to delight all our guests. (In many of the letters we received when Stephen died, his Turkish coffee was mentioned.) Years ago, he had been shown the recipe by a beautiful Lebanese girlfriend of his brother Tom.

Recently, my godson, Ben Gregson-Williams, son of Philippa Grey-Edwards, who painted the delightful portrait of Stephen on this book cover, wrote to me, saying:

> *I've just been thinking about Stephen. I have never forgotten him making us Turkish cardamom coffee, the theatre and ritual involved in the grinding of the coffee and cardamom, the tilting of the little copper saucepan to encourage the sediment into one place and the careful pouring to avoid disturbing that sediment . . . and that taste!*

Stephen used to buy the Turkish coffee beans from the covered market in Oxford. I had ordered, from the Algerian Coffee Stores in Soho, two copper pots – one large, one small. It was always a pleasure to watch Stephen, at the end of a meal, carefully, and proudly, pouring the coffee into some very small porcelain pots (a delightful present we had received from MoMA in New York), our guests, unfailingly, entranced.*

*TURKISH (or GREEK) COFFEE RECIPE
(As shown to Stephen by Leila, a Lebanese girlfriend of his brother Tom)

Brass or copper pot: 4' base

Fill to ¾ with water
Add 4 teaspoons sugar
Bring to boil on kitchen hob

Remove from hob
Add 3 heaped tablespoons of *pulverised* coffee ('Finely' ground is not fine enough)
Stir

Put back on hob (low heat) until the coffee froths up to the top of pot
Remove *immediately*. (It must NOT boil)
Repeat this two more times

Add a very little cold water. Stir
Leave to settle for about 9 minutes, with pot <u>tilted at an angle </u>so all the grounds
go to the bottom
Pour out coffee, making sure no grounds have come into the (very small) cups
(Stephen heats the cups in advance with boiling water, but this may be too much.)

Amounts can vary according to taste: it can be 'glyky' (sweet) or 'metrio' (medium)
(Unsweetened, Stephen says, it is only used to cure a hangover)
This should be enough for 5 or 6 people

Chapter 8
Birth of Isabel (Zazie)

On 25 April 1979, our daughter, Zazie, 9lbs, was born at 4.30pm at the Radcliffe Infirmary in Oxford. ('Teatime!' said Stephen, proudly.) We named her Isabel. I had wanted a French name and, when we discovered that the French nickname for Isabel was Zazie, we were delighted. She was a most beautiful and healthy baby. Stephen was in the delivery room when she was born. He thought she was the most exquisite human being he'd ever seen – and was to think that till the end of his life. Stephen's deep love for Zazie was the greatest joy for me.

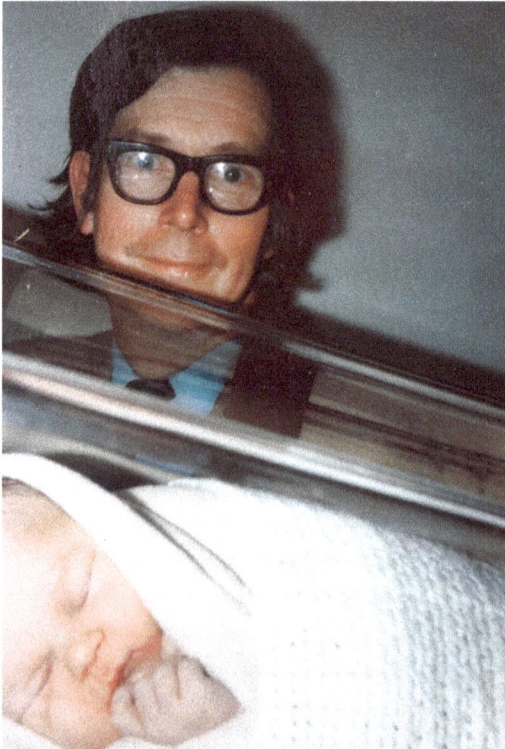

Stephen with Zazie,
newborn, 25 April 1979

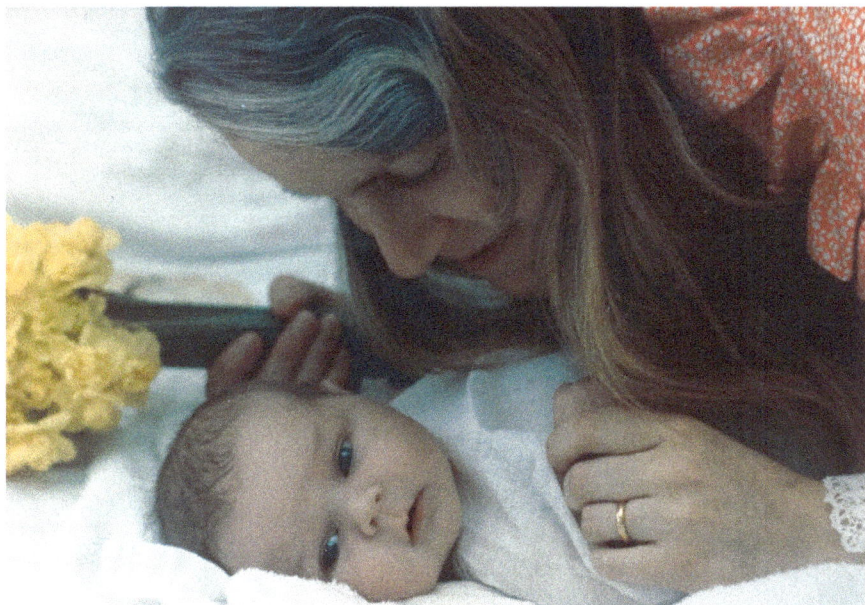

Me with Zazie, five days old

Our vicar's splendid wife, Elizabeth Evans, mother of six, came to help me when we came home.

'All I need is some gripe juice and a washing line,' she said.

As I'd never had a washing line – I imagined they were things you had in Naples, although I'd never been there – Norman and I rigged one up in the orchard, near a pond I had just discovered, tying it to a huge walnut tree.

Looking through the Baby Book I kept for Zazie, I see I wrote the following shortly after her birth:

I found the responsibility for a baby quite, quite terrifying. I've never in fact been so frightened in all my life. It just seemed to completely weigh me down with fear. I thought of the future and of our ages and of this selfish and indulgent thing we'd done – to have this beautiful, perfect, good little baby and what could we possibly give her? I felt it was so, so wrong and sat and cried, holding her, for hours. Elizabeth told me not to cross my bridges till I came to them. I must have crossed a hundred in those few days (and for many months thereafter).

I was thirty-nine when Zazie was born. Maybe, many new mothers feel equally inadequate?

Years later, I was to say to my friend Julia Tugendhat, by then a family therapist, that I felt we had failed Zazie. 'But, Freddie, we *all* fail our children in one way or another,' she replied, which I found very comforting.

I had been asked if we were going to have a nanny.

'What?' I replied. 'A beastly woman who'd say I had to let my baby cry to exercise her lungs.'

Instead, when our daughter was two, we engaged a dear girl from the next village called Polly.

Polly was sixteen, the eldest of five siblings. She was just what I wanted, with no ideas of her own: placid and calm, all the things I was not. When feeding Zazie, she used to play 'trains' with food on the spoon ('choo, choo, choo ...'), a revelation to me – and it worked. Polly came with us everywhere: to Greece, to Sussex, to Hertfordshire. We loved her.

Stephen could not have been a more loving father. Whenever Zazie cried, which was rarely, as I wouldn't ever let her cry – not now (in 2023) thought correct, I believe, as babies are supposed to be allowed to 'self-soothe' – we would both gaze at her in the cot, Stephen saying seriously, 'It's either water or milk that she needs.'

My stalwart friend Marjory said, one day, as I ran to Zazie crying in the orchard in her pram,

Jean Dawkins, Stephen (with Zazie in sling) and me walking in Over Norton Park, 1979

'Freddie, never run to your baby.'

'I will *always* run to my baby,' I fiercely replied.

As for anyone saying babies needed to cry to exercise their lungs, this put me into an apoplectic rage. Even in shops, if I heard a baby crying I'd go up to the mother and ask if I could help. A nurse at the John Radcliffe Hospital in Oxford said I must have been allowed to cry a lot as a baby. I asked my darling mother, who said, yes, it was the fashion. When my sister was born three years later, the fashion had changed!

When Stephen changed Zazie's nappy, which he did every morning, I could tell whilst sitting in the room below whether it was a dirty nappy or not as, if dirty, he'd practically run across the room to the nappy bucket. If not dirty, he'd walk very slowly. (Why wasn't the bucket underneath the changing table, I've just wondered?)

Zazie's Christening took place at Little Compton church. The end of July. She was three months old. Robin Waterfield was Zazie's godfather; Julia Tugendhat and Valerie Clutterbuck were her splendid godmothers. It was a memorable occasion, which meant a great deal to Stephen and to his brother Charles, who conducted the service. Elizabeth Evens washed and starched the beautiful old family robe, and Stephen's Aunt Audrey (Iyum) reassured me about the garden. 'Darling, all you need is the grass cut and the edges trimmed. No one will notice the weeds.' Iyum did the church flowers, magnificently, and Nini saw to the salads, the strawberries, the shelling of Norman's broad beans . . . Both she and Iyum were the greatest support, and Zazie, so easy and happy . . .

Stephen holding Zazie
after the christening

Our first party outing since Zazie's birth, Nini babysitting

The Pram: This was a problem. We had a beautiful old-fashioned pram in which I'd wrap Zazie up securely and off Stephen would go, wheeling her so proudly, beaming so happily. I thought all was well until neighbours started ringing me up, saying, 'Freddie, you do know that Stephen walks with the pram in the middle of the road, don't you?'

I tackled him about this but he said that according to the Highways Act of 1835, one was forbidden from pushing a wheeled vehicle on a pavement.

(It was rather the same when we walked in London before we were married. I remember one warm sunny summer's evening in a pretty, leafy residential street in Chelsea, both so happy, my suggesting to Stephen that he didn't walk in the middle of the road as he might be run over; that it might be better if he walked on the pavement.

'Why shouldn't I? No one's going to run *me* over.'

That was the only arrogant thing I ever heard Stephen say. Maybe walking with a much younger woman had gone to his head?)

Zazie was very pretty, with auburn hair and enormous blue eyes. And so easy. She adored Mustoe, our untrained golden Labrador dog, and this love was mutual. Zazie would spend a lot of time sitting on Mustoe, talking and reading, treating him much like a large cushion. When she was newborn, Mustoe lay under her pram when it was outside. In every childhood photograph, there is Mustoe, right beside her.

Up until Zazie's birth, Mustoe had been our baby. We had no idea how to deal with a large puppy. (I had even put a bar of chocolate in the hall table drawer before I went to the hospital to have Zazie. 'Darling, this is for Mustoe when we get back so that he won't feel so dethroned,' dethronement being one of my permanent life anxieties. Alas, amidst the excitement of bringing home our beautiful baby, we somehow managed to forget that bar of chocolate, only discovering it many months later, fairly mouldy.)

Mustoe chewed everyone's handbags when they came to supper (having left them on the sofa or near their chair whilst we ate), humped any woman who wore red and was generally a complete nightmare. Stephen and I decided to take him to puppy training classes at Chipping Norton where, after one session, the terrifying instructress said to me, 'You might as well give up. You two will never be able to train a dog.'

How right she was! Yet, when Zazie was born, Mustoe was transformed.

Under the apple tree with Mustoe

More Expulsions: Being expelled from the puppy training class reminds me of being expelled from a rather smart little private nursery school near Moreton-in-Marsh to which I took Zazie when she was about two or three.

Zazie was very happy there but I could tell that the very nice nursery teacher didn't approve of my plan to send Zazie to the village school rather than to the nearby smart prep school, Kitebrook, and, sure enough, after four days, I received a letter saying that she didn't think her nursery was the right one for us.

Another expulsion was from the ballet class in Stow-on-the-Wold at much the same time. All was going along happily until the children were told to 'Be little bunnies' and hide under their mother's chair. They all rushed to do this but Zazie said she didn't want to. I reassured her, 'It doesn't matter at all, darling, just come and sit on the floor beside me.'

But a terrifying old woman, mother of the teacher, came up to us, frowning, and said, 'Why don't you just make her do it?' which astonished me. That was the end of ballet classes.

Something Zazie remembers with great affection was Stephen showing her, when she was about five, the star constellations at night, drawing the curtains in her bedroom, explaining it to her in the greatest detail, Zazie entranced.

Nini's Visits: My French mother, Marie-Madeleine, whom we called Nini (pronounced knee-knee), used to come and stay with us regularly. For the last years of her life, when she became too frail to renovate houses, something she was so good at doing, she lived happily with my sister, Michie, and her husband, John Herbert, at Much Hadham Hall, near Bishop's Stortford. There, my sister made Nini a comfortable flat at the top of the house. It was a perfect arrangement, seeing my sister every day, and my two nieces – whom she loved dearly – whenever they were home. Michie could not have done more for Nini, and I will always be grateful to her and to John for the love and support they showed Nini for a great many years.

Nini would come to us for several months at a time. This was a small way of helping to share her care and it brought us great joy. We loved her visits and much looked forward to them. Zazie adored her and would rush home from school to see her. Ditto Black Cat, who would spend most of his day on Nini's bed. Nini tended to stay in her room, coming down to a sherry and supper at about 6pm when she would sit with Stephen by the fire in the sitting room or, in summer, in the garden, wearing a straw hat and meeting our friends. Kate Morgan Hildyard's daughters, Sophie, Emily and Polly, used to babysit if we had to go out. Nini loved their company, as she did that of our vicar's son, Jonathan Evans, aged about ten, who enchanted her with his good looks, especially his smile; something she never ceased to mention.

The birth of Zazie gave Nini great happiness; a late joy and one she treasured. Frequent letters, photos, annual summer holidays with her at her house on the lle de Ré … We were beyond grateful to have Nini in our lives.

Nini feeding Zazie

Nini at Pilbridge on our first Christmas Day with Zazie, 1979

But Stephen mystified her. What exactly was his work as an archivist? Did it make any money? Nini's dream son-in-law would have been a highly successful banker with a very large 1920s house in the Surrey stockbroker belt with electronic gates, two new cars in the drive, a large tree-filled, maintenance-free garden, someone who dashed up to London on the 6am train, returning at about 8pm each evening, making an absolute fortune ... Alas, mercifully for me, not a description of dear Stephen at all.

Nini died peacefully of old age in 1995, aged ninety-two. Thinking of her has always been immensely painful for me. I loved her more than anyone else. We had all three (Nini, Michie and I) been through a sad childhood during which Nini did her utmost to make us feel loved and safe. She never shouted, was never cross. No mother could have done more. But I did let her down as an adult by not being cleverer at dealing with money, something Nini considered more important than anything else.

Nini was not to know of our eventual happy move to Caudle Green or Stephen's Latin translations, which I doubt would have impressed her. ('How many people will buy such books?' she'd have wondered.) And she didn't know about Zazie going to UCL and, later, entering the film world.

The Village School: Until she was eight, Zazie went to the village school, which charmed Stephen and Tom, Tom saying, after one sports day, how splendid he thought it was that every child received a prize. Zazie made many friends, our life circling around endless tea parties, birthday celebrations, outings, splendid Christmas plays that the school put on, walks and informative hedgerow tours ... I loved the idea that all the children from the village were there together; so did Stephen, who used to walk Zazie proudly to school every morning along a foot-path beside a field. I said to him, 'Darling, you will tell Zazie about the changing crops and seasons, won't you?' Stephen frowned and more or less said that he couldn't possibly talk to Zazie as the responsibility of getting her safely to school was so great – that they had to cross a main road – and that Zazie's safety was what he had to focus on.

Stephen didn't actually consider Zazie's education. It wasn't his fault. He really didn't know about schools and learning, his own education having been so privileged. When Zazie once asked him if he had any tips about revising for her A-levels, he looked bemused, obviously never having had to revise for any exam himself. And I was no help, either. We both just wanted Zazie to be happy. Eventually, she weekly boarded at Headington School in Oxford, (home for three nights a week), then at Cheltenham Ladies' College, which she much enjoyed and, finally, went to University College London (UCL) to read Philosophy, all entirely on her own merit and her own hard work, with no advice or suggestions from her parents. (We'd go to the parents' evenings at Cheltenham Ladies' where Stephen, I remember, tended to look at the portraits on the wall, paying no attention to what Zazie's teacher was saying about his daughter's work, however hard I nudged him.)

Friends: I, too, made many good friends in Little Compton, including dear Kate Hildyard (to whom I have written a tribute below). Angela Brown had been a BBC graphic designer, was sophisticated and the greatest fun; she had two small children, Alice and Edward, of whom I was very fond and who frequently came to see me; the Thins, living on the other side of the road, Zazie playing endlessly with Emily and the twins in their stream, holidaying with them in Portugal, and dear Liz Drury, who did – and still does – a very great deal for so many and who encouraged Zazie to ride. Lora and Roger Amos were arty and fun, their two daughters, Annika and Clare, often playing with Zazie. Now in St Ives, we've had the happiest, most spoiling of visits to them there, serenaded by Roger on his flute and hearing about St Ives' Jazz Club.

We much admired Alec Reed and his beautiful wife, Adrianne, who had bought Little Compton Manor (now called Reed Business School), where Stephen had lived as a child (and to whose archive collection we recently so gladly contributed many papers). Alec started Reed Employment Agency and became, many successful years later, a great philanthropist, founding Womankind and Ethiopiaid, amongst other charities – always with Adrianne's support and love behind him. (Ethiopiaid was a charity about which Stephen felt very strongly. Whenever we received a notice in the post, he would say, 'Darling, we *must* send something to those poor hungry people.' Somehow, it moved him deeply. At Stephen's funeral, we asked if the collection could be in aid of both Syde and Chastleton churches as well as Ethiopiaid.)

Tribute to Kate Hildyard (1950-2024)

Kate was one of my most precious friends. She and her first husband, Arden Morgan, an agricultural consultant, had three daughters – Sophie, Emily and Polly – all of whom went to Little Compton village school with Zazie. Later, we shared hideously early morning lifts to the school bus in Chipping Norton, which then dropped them off at their various secondary schools in Oxford.

Emily (Morgan) was the fearless and much-admired ITN health reporter during the COVID crisis. Tragically, Emily died suddenly in May 2023, aged forty-five, within six weeks of lung cancer being diagnosed. She left her husband and two little girls, Aggie, aged seven and Etta, nine.

Polly (Morgan) has become a well-known artist using the medium of taxidermy, is married to the YBA, Matt Collishaw and has two young sons, Clifford, eight and Bruce, six.

After her divorce, Kate married Robin Hildyard, a distinguished V&A ceramic expert whom she had known since 1968. She and Robin lived happily near Moreton-in-Marsh for over twenty years, devoting time and energy to their nine grandchildren. (Sophie's two delightful sons, both having been head boys, no less, are already enormously tall, beautifully mannered, handsome young men of whom Kate was so proud, as she was of their sister, Sasha and, indeed, of *all* her grandchildren as well as her two step-grandchildren.)

The Oxford Ceramics Group was always a great pleasure, as were trips abroad in Robin's splendid 1925 vintage car with the Frazer Nash Car Club.

But, sadly, Kate, having found some comfort in caring once more for their beautiful garden developed, very suddenly, a rare bacterial heart infection. After ten days in a coma, Kate could no longer be saved. She was seventy-four. It was April 2024, eleven months after Emily's death.

Kate, beautiful, uncritical, though highly perceptive, thoughtful, utterly modest, always there when one needed her wise and calm

Robin and Kate

advice, strong and brave – no words can do her justice – was the most superb wife, mother and grandmother – and quite the *very* best friend anyone could have. We shall all miss her most dreadfully.

Jane Brabyn was a very special friend – and the greatest fun. We had been introduced to her by Wendy and Eric Goudie, gentlemen farmers in Little Compton. I remember Wendy's daughter saying, firmly, at the lunch, 'We are *agri*-culture,' whereas Jane was 'culture'. It could not have been a happier introduction.

Somewhat eccentric, the granddaughter of Sir Thomas Beecham, music was in Jane's blood. She held splendid concerts – usually in aid of a charity – at her beautiful old house near Shipston-on-Stour. We went to as many as we could, though actually getting into the house to hear the music was quite amusing. There was no question of going through the elegant <u>front</u> door but, no, for some reason, we all had to queue up, patiently, outside a muddy back entrance, surrounded by piles of logs under a rusty corrugated roof, various dustbins, bags of compost and fertiliser, an old wheelbarrow, a few cracked terracotta pots, a washing line ... those sort of things. (I remember hearing one guest say to another, waving her hand at it all, 'Of course, she does this on purpose ...') The ultimate pleasure, before we were allowed into the house, was the sight of an enormous Tibetan flag tied to a nearby tree, waving energetically in the wind. I never thought to ask Jane why a *Tibetan* flag? (She rang me a few days ago. I should have said, 'By the way, why did you fly that Tibetan flag?' ... but I didn't.)

If Jane had cooked a splendid meal, as she did, for instance, at Christmas, and we had all said enthusiastically how particularly delicious it was, Jane would invariably ask, anxiously, looking worried, 'Is it all right?' This faux-modest response impressed me deeply. I always hoped I would remember to say exactly the same thing when I'd cooked something especially splendid but, sadly, I always forgot.

It was Jane, often with daughter Lowdy, a good friend of Zazie, who encouraged us to go with her on many trips abroad, some of which I have described later on in this book; Jane, who, above all, adored

Stephen – and who could make him laugh in a way that few others ever could.

At Little Compton, we had so much for which to be grateful. We had doggy friends, and children friends, church friends and WI friends. It also meant so much to Stephen – to live in the same village and surrounding area that his family had lived in for generations. But, in trying to do everything, I mismanaged so much, achieving so little; endless house moves, endless brainwaves ... When we left that village twenty years later, no one was sadder than Stephen and me. For months afterwards, every time anyone mentioned Little Compton, I burst into tears. I had learnt what a very great privilege it was to live amongst a community of diverse people who accepted you, and even loved you, with all your faults and failings. This is what a family does, if you are lucky, and a precious family was what the village of Little Compton had become for me.

Chapter 9

Moving to Woodfield House, Caudle Green

In 1994, our lives were to change yet again. We had had seven years of litigation (an unwise pursuit on my part) over a family house, Casa Forbes, on Lake Orta in Italy that had been left to me by my father in his will. In the end, I realised that I would not win this case. The legal fees were enormous. We had to sell our own house, as well.

Mentioning this to our friend Emma Tennant, she suggested we go and look at her aunt's house in Caudle Green, near Cheltenham, a fifty-minute drive from Little Compton. (The aunt was Pamela Jackson, one of the Mitford sisters. Emma was the daughter of Debo, the Duchess of Devonshire, Pamela's younger sister.) Pamela had only just recently died and the house was empty.*

Zazie and I drove there one sunny May day. Pure heaven. Who could criticise such a house in such a setting, surrounded by fields, views, valleys, wildlife, the ancient Miserden woods ... six bedrooms and an exquisite garden ... and a walled *kitchen* garden. We told Emma that we loved it. She asked if we'd like to rent it. We sold our house in Little Compton and moved to Woodfield within a few months. (I was fifty-four and had, finally, got my driving licence, vital in this little remote corner.)

Thus began the happiest years of my life – twenty-three years in a glorious house in a tiny hamlet. (I discovered that a hamlet is a village that doesn't have a church.) No one could have asked for more.

---

*Woodfield House was the childhood home of the DNA pioneer, Sir Frederick Sanger, (Fred), British biochemist who twice won the Nobel Prize (1958 and 1980). Fred is buried at Syde church, half a mile from Caudle Green.

Woodfield House, Caudle Green

Garden view from upstairs

By now, I knew how to behave in a village. Had learnt the ropes, got the hang of it... but I did miss Little Compton very much indeed. At one point, we were invited to live at nearby Chastleton House (by then owned by the National Trust), not exactly as caretakers, but just to occupy the house and be welcoming, if necessary. Stephen had helped write the guidebook and was a well-known local expert on its history. I felt it was a way of getting back to that little corner, which I was mourning so deeply. Yet at the last minute, when the National Trust had so kindly let me choose carpets and bookshelves, I got cold feet. It was the size of the house as we left it one winter's evening, looking back and seeing it as we drove away, lit up in the darkness, and the thought of how dreadfully impractical we both were: what would we do in an emergency? What if Stephen in the night accidentally walked into those thick red ropes that cordoned off forbidden rooms, which would set an alarm ringing? Instead, we stayed on at Caudle Green ... and how grateful I am that we did so but, equally, how grateful I was to have had Chastleton House offered to us as a possible refuge.

Woodfield House is Queen Anne, though one side is probably much older. As soon as you step into the house, there is a feeling that this is home: not grand or large but somehow welcoming and warm. There are stables – in which Emma allowed us to keep furniture and trunks full of precious family papers – fields to walk through, an adjacent barn for logs – and for yet more papers . . .

Emma had so generously left in the house much of her aunt's furniture and books, all of which gave us great pleasure. And some of her own rag rugs and very lovely botanical paintings, too – more pleasure.

(Maybe you need to have been brought up by an eccentric writer father in a tiny thatched cottage deep in those Hertfordshire woods, with no electricity or running water, to appreciate the gift of such a house and setting which, though not your own, you were fortunate and privileged enough to make your own for a great many years.)

The hamlet of Caudle Green (twenty-one houses) has proved to be a curious *mélange* of interesting people, including several working at GCHQ in Cheltenham.

We have had amongst us in the last forty years, a retired chaplain to the late Queen, teachers, keen bird watchers, a senior judge, nurses, retired army officers, the bursar of an Oxford college, a Mitford sister, excellent horse riders, a fantasy book illustrator, a roof tiler, many splendid gardeners, lawyers, several doctors, a film producer, musicians and the retired headmistress of Cheltenham Ladies' College, all supportive and discreetly willing to help one another, if necessary.

Our nearest church is enchanting: small, Norman, Grade I listed, it is at Syde, half a mile up a hill. There, we have an even smaller but nonetheless diverse group of residents, equally splendid, all of whom contribute much to the church and to the community, and where there is the added advantage of regular international chamber music concerts hosted by the uniquely generous Syde Manor owners, Penny Wright and Andrew Neubauer.

Claire Jardine, a hugely helpful member of this little hamlet, as is her husband, Andrew, is currently writing a book (with photographs) that will celebrate the history of the houses and their residents in both Caudle Green and Syde.

Each one of us really does know and appreciate how fortunate we are to live here, how magical this unspoilt corner is in summer. We know, too, how very cold and icy it is in winter.

Soon after moving, I became aware that Woodfield was going to be a *shared* house in many ways. On our first morning, our neighbour, Julian Leeds, who was to become a dear friend and a practical lifeline for Stephen and me, came to our back door saying that Gerald, the Wood-field gardener, had told him that he could pick some broad beans in the kitchen garden. That was the very first inkling of how we were going to share the kitchen garden, for a start ...

Gerald was splendid. He had already worked at Woodfield for Emma's aunt, Pam Jackson, for many years. Emma kept him on most gratefully until he died in 2010. The garden was immaculate. He loved it – and so did we, and anyone coming to the house. It was so easy for Gerald, living next door. He'd come over on summer evenings to do some tidying up or weeding, always giving us vegetables and fruit as they became ready. We were spoilt beyond words.

Gerald was a deeply silent man, as was Stephen. I am really not sure that they ever *really* spoke to one another at all in all those twenty-three years. I did my best but my lack of horticultural knowledge was so great, I didn't contribute much. Without actually saying anything, we sort of divided the garden up and I was allowed to buy – and ask Gerald to kindly plant – all sorts of fun flowers, roses, even trees, including a beautiful cherry, *Prunus Tai-haku*. This worked so well. Gerald was extremely patient both with me and with Stephen's herb patch, which meant a great deal to Stephen but which, sadly, was never weeded and became a complete eyesore. (Stephen would pick vast amounts of herbs for me, putting them near the cooker in the hope that I would include them in some delicious meal ...)

Emma would often come and stay, which was always a great pleasure – meeting our friends, enjoying the garden, seeing Gerald and Gladys. Very keen on history – and a great admirer of Stephen – Emma was so good at encouraging him to talk. Stephen was not initially easy to speak to in that he didn't ever start a conversation. Toby and Emma would drive down from Scotland, Emma saying, almost before she took her coat off,

'Stephen, I've been longing to tell you that I heard on the radio the other day that King … was nearly beheaded in 16 … because he had … That can't possibly be true, can it?'

'Oh no,' Stephen would reply. 'That is not right at all. What actually happened was …'

… and then would follow a lengthy historical discussion, all of us sitting around the kitchen table, Toby and I slightly rolling our eyes and focusing on our supper, but which discussion was greatly enjoyable for Emma and Stephen.

Pipe Lids and Hedgehogs by Gerald Stewart (The Choir Press, 2009): One cold grey winter's day, I bought at Woolworths a lined notepad and pen and took them to Gerald next door, saying, 'Gerald, *please* will you write your life story.'

He did! It took him three dark winters, when there was no gardening for him to do, writing at his desk in the corner of his sitting room. When finished, I had it privately published by The Choir Press, the Duchess of Devonshire having kindly written a Foreword. Emma came down to open the book launch at Woodfield, which was a huge triumph and great fun, resulting in all the 125 copies we had had printed being sold; Gerald and his family, astonished and delighted.

Emma Tennant with Gerald Stewart at the Woodfield book launch of his Pipe Lids and Hedgehogs

Parties: Two memorable parties took place at Chastleton House, courtesy of the National Trust: one for Stephen's eightieth birthday and another for his ninetieth. Fun bands, fun speeches – read out jovially by Colin Russell – delicious food, sunshine ... Remembering them both, I am aware of what a privilege it was to be allowed to have those parties, there, in the beautifully kept gardens with a tour of that enchanting Jacobean house included in the invitation ...

We had moved to Caudle Green in May, a particularly glorious month in the country. By Christmas, I felt I had met most neighbours and could have a party. Gerald was Father Christmas, coming in from the darkness through the front door, ringing Stephen's mother's old school bell and distributing presents to the children by the log fire. We sang carols. I was blissfully happy. After that, there were many parties, Zazie often coming down from London, where she was studying at UCL, everyone kindly bringing food, drink – Stephen and I merely providing the space. Speeches, usually by (Canon) Andrew Bowden, our dearly loved neighbour (and retired chaplain to the late Queen), of whom we are all so hugely proud, thanking, welcoming ... Nothing before or since – other than my daughter's marriage and my two grandsons – has given me more pleasure than living at Woodfield and sharing that house.

Andrew Bowden talking Greek icons with Toby Tennant

Julian Leeds and Jane Brabyn

*Philippa Grey-Edwards, right, who painted the delightful portrait of Stephen
that we have put on the cover of this book, with Julia Tugendhat*

Stephen (with napkin chain) and Colin Russell

Puddings: My culinary repertoire was the best at that time that it's ever been, but that, sadly, is not saying too much. *However*, a chocolate biscuit pudding that changed my life – and the lives of those who ate it – was a Chocolate Crunch Christmas Pudding. This pudding, by Josceline Dimbleby in 1978, was brought to a party at Woodfield many years ago by my dear doctor, one-time Primrose Hill friend, Elisabeth Beverley, whose gardens, interiors and recipes never fail to look as though they have come straight out of *House & Garden*. Everyone swooned. I stole the recipe and, ever since, Chocolate Crunch has been my go-to cold pudding, one that can be made in any shape or size, filled with fruit, flowers, nuts or just flat and unadorned ... a pudding joy!

The Pig and the Pink Striped Pyjamas: For Stephen's ninety-sixth birthday party, I suggested he could perhaps make a short speech about an amusing incident in his childhood. He frowned and looked worried; he couldn't think of anything remotely funny. Days went by ... still no incidents that would make us all laugh. I despaired. There must have been some slightly comical occurrence, surely? Something very silly that one of the three brothers had done by accident? No. Then, suddenly, Stephen said, 'Well, I could tell the story of the Pig and the Pink Striped Pyjamas.'

The story went like this: As a small child, Stephen had always wanted some pink striped pyjamas. When he was about four, his mother bought him a pair. Stephen was delighted. After a while, they had to go to the wash. They were then hung out on the line to dry when, very sadly, all of a sudden, the washerwoman's pig came up, saw the pyjamas and ... *ate them*! And this sorry tale doesn't end there ... the pig *died!* Of *indigestion*! Everyone at the party roared and clapped. It was a great success. (Stephen's father never got over his bad luck in having to buy his son another pair of pyjamas *and* buy the washerwoman another pig.)

Stephen telling cousin Jean Dawkins about the Pink Striped Pyjamas speech that he had made at his ninety-sixth birthday party, February 2016

Ear Trumpets: For parties, Stephen used to take an ear trumpet. This was quite fun. It ought to have been a beautiful old tortoiseshell one, but, sadly, it was made of black plastic. It had been broken in several places and mended by Stephen with strips of thick brown tape, which now held it together. Stephen would wear it over his shoulder, casually, like a duffel bag.

The idea of the ear trumpet was a very good one in that it meant Stephen (very deaf) could hear what someone was saying. The problem arose when he didn't remove it after the person had finished speaking. This was quite embarrassing, the person having to say, 'Stephen, I've finished now' or some such, after which Stephen would take it down and attach it to the next person who wanted to speak to him.

Charles Keen and Julia Tugendhat, after lunch at Woodfield, remembering their time at Oxford

Driving: Stephen's driving was always a problem. (Mine was no better.) Never having had to pass a test, he must have learnt to drive in about 1938. He drove very slowly and very carefully. Cars would queue up behind us, getting crosser and crosser. On one occasion, we had been to see our doctor and, having turned onto a very busy road, we then had to turn left onto a quiet country lane.

'Darling, you will indicate that we're turning left, won't you, so that the driver behind us knows.'

Stephen frowned. 'Why should I? It's none of his business.'

Stephen didn't notice the makes or shapes or colours of cars, either. He didn't know one from another; they were all the same to him. (I am now exactly like that.)

'Cars are just a means of transport,' he explained.

Windows: Stephen never looked out of windows.

'Either I am inside or outside,' he would say.

When we were first married, he'd get up and draw the curtains.

'What's the weather like?' I'd ask.

He'd frown and look puzzled ... He never actually knew whether it was raining/snowing/sunny/foggy till he stepped outside. When I met him, he wore the same clothes all the year round. If I said something like, 'I don't think we'll be able to drive [in the little old brown Hillman Imp] to Suffolk tomorrow because they forecast snow,' he wouldn't understand.

The worst journey we had was to the funeral of a distant cousin of Stephen, Valerie Tempest, in Kent, in 1978. Thick snow and we had to collect the service sheets at Bourton-on-the-Water as a little detour. Cars were stranded on all sides of every road we took, but we ploughed on very, very slowly in the trusty Hillman, Stephen perfectly calm, as always, me beside myself with worry. After about six hours, we got there; the service was just beginning. Valerie's ninety-six-year-old sister, Hazel Budgett, greeted us warmly. We had made it. The trouble was we had to then get back. We went to London to stay with Tom as a shorter option.

'Have you ever been so tired in all your life?' I asked him.

'Yes,' he said, 'at Bletchley when the next person on the [decoding] shift didn't turn up, so one had to do sixteen hours in one stint.'

A few years ago, our clergyman friend, Jeremy Francis, and his wife, Anna, kindly took Stephen to Gloucester Cathedral for a service. Stephen was about ninety-four. It began to snow heavily whilst they were there. Jeremy, quite a bit younger than Stephen, was very worried about Stephen falling down. After the service, they gingerly walked him back to the car. Then, Jeremy, driving very slowly in the heavy snow, reached the safety of Caudle Green and our front door.

'I was so worried that Stephen might fall,' Jeremy said to me.

'Darling, how was the snow?' I asked Stephen, later.

'Snow? What snow? But I'm *very* worried about Jeremy. He was walking *so* slowly.'

Jeremy Francis and Stephen, deep in prayerful thought

Asperger's Syndrome: In the 1980s and 1990s, the syndrome known as Asperger started to be written about. I didn't take much notice of it but, slowly, a few friends began to suggest that Stephen might have a touch of this syndrome. In 1998, when Stephen was seventy-eight, a book on the subject was written by Tony Attwood, which I bought (*Asperger's Syndrome*, Jessica Kingsley Publishers). There were many aspects of the syndrome that seemed familiar, many that did not.

I gave a copy to Stephen to read. I can't remember what I said exactly. He was in his study. After a while, I became quite agitated to think I was giving this darling man a book about a syndrome that he might have – yet had had no idea of it until now. Such an unkind and unnecessary thing to do to a very old man. How could I? I rushed into the study, saying, 'Darling, I don't think Asperger's is really like you at all ...' and took the book away from him. He was very calm and not in the least perturbed.

'Well, yes, darling, I do think it is quite like me, and I also think it is quite like *you*.'

I was so relieved. Giving it to him had done no harm. And his comment confirms the opinion of many that we all have a small bit of Asperger's in our psyche, some more than others. And maybe now ADHD, autism and so much else ...

I remember, in order to save space, starting to write little notes in shorthand in the diary we kept by the telephone to remind myself of things to do. Prune roses ... Pay milkman ... that sort of thing. Stephen, noticing this and without saying a word, started writing little notes in Greek ...

Elisabeth Beverley introducing us to Chocolate Crunch Christmas Pudding.
December 2009

Chapter 10

Translating Latin Books for Oxford University Press (OUP)

1988. Before we left Little Compton, our good friend Jane Brabyn had invited us to dinner. She thought we'd enjoy meeting a retired doctor friend, Christopher Wharton, and his wife. At the end of the meal, Christopher (a Fellow of the Royal College of Physicians) asked Stephen if he would consider translating *Adenographia* ('Anatomy of the Glands') written in Latin in 1656 by a medical ancestor of his, Thomas Wharton (1614–1673). Wharton was an English physician and anatomist, best known for his 'descriptions of the submandibular duct [one of the salivary ducts] and Wharton's jelly of the umbilical cord'. There you have it! Stephen said he'd be very glad to learn more ...

Seven years later, in 1995, Stephen finished the translation. I typed it up and contacted Oxford University Press to see if they would consider publishing it. They did, in 1996, most beautifully, with the Latin on the left page, the English on the right. And so began a fruitful and happy relationship with OUP. (I was amused on reading the Appendix in *Adenographia* about a friend of Dr Wharton who, in 1673, seeks his opinion as to whether her son should pursue a career in medicine. Wharton keenly discourages such an idea, giving a long list of the disadvantages of dealing with patients and, above all, with fellow doctors!)

Adenographia was the first commission of three Latin translations that Stephen was asked to do, each one taking seven years to complete. Described in a review by Professor Harold Cook of the Wellcome Foundation as 'one of the most important works on anatomy published in England in the mid-seventeenth century', he wrote,

We are indebted to Stephen Freer for this excellent translation of Thomas Wharton's work on the glands, and to Dr Christopher Wharton, a descendant of Thomas, for commissioning Freer's work.

Sadly, Christopher Wharton died before the book was published, but we enjoyed several meetings with him to discuss the work, and I know he was very happy with Stephen's suggestions and ideas.

After the publication of *Adenographia* in 1995* (we were now living at Woodfield House in Caudle Green), two OUP editors came to lunch. Standing in Stephen's study, one of them said, 'Stephen: you can translate *any* Latin book at all and we will publish it.'

I thought, initially, perhaps something to do with cookery, a subject that had become so topical and of such great interest. English cooking – and recipes – in the last fifty years had changed beyond recognition, now so sophisticated – thanks in part to Elisabeth David and her foreign travels. I imagined discovering a wonderfully old recipe book and text that could have been great fun to translate – and been very popular.

Another subject that was rapidly gaining great television attention was gardening. I sought advice from two garden designers/writers who were near neighbours: Rosemary Verey and Mary Keen. Both were very helpful, with splendid ideas. But, at the same time, we heard that a professor (Dr Arthur Cain) at Liverpool University had suggested that *Philosophia Botanica*, written in 1751 by the Swedish botanist Carl Linnaeus, was a very important work, a translation of which would be very welcome indeed.

And so we went from medicine to botany. A biography I found enormously helpful and interesting was Wilfred Blunt's *The Compleat Naturalist – A Life of Linnaeus*, given to us by Tom. (Wilfred Blunt was Tom's art master at Eton.) This book brought Linnaeus to life for me: details of his childhood, his house in Uppsala, his wife, his children, his trip to Lapland, including his sketches, his long career, and many splendid colour plates and photographs. It was – and is – a great joy.

---

* Thomas Wharton's *Adenographia*, translated by Stephen Freer. OUP, 1996

Seven years later, Stephen's translation of Linnaeus's *Philosophia Botanica* was finished. It was published by OUP in 2003* to the kindest reviews that made me weep. 'A gift to the world', said one. Showing them to Stephen, he remained completely calm, probably noticing some tiny error in the reviewer's text but too polite to mention it. I do hope those reviews made all that hard work rewarding and uplifting for him.

OUP had asked me to contact potential reviewers myself. They actually said, 'You would do it so much better than we would.'

I had no idea about botanical journals, but the Linnean Society, which became a lifeline, the dynamic Gina Douglas never failing to be hugely helpful, gave me a list of possible societies and journals that would undoubtedly be only too glad to review *Philosophia*. The Linnean Society (which, of course, I had never even heard of) is one of five learned societies in the Royal Academy courtyard and, on our first visit there, the RA Summer Exhibition was in full swing. Gina was unlocking cupboards with precious keys held around her waist, just as Stephen's mother used to do, producing ancient tomes of great botanical importance whilst also introducing us to one of Britain's most eminent botanists, Dr William T. Stearn, but, sadly, all I could think of was escaping to the Summer Exhibition next door.

There were fifteen reviews in total, all heaping praise on the book. The botanical editors of the learned societies I contacted were unfailingly a great delight to work with, so pleased to hear about the book, so eager to review it. I remember in particular Dr Philip Oswald, of the Archives of Natural History, who became a good friend. Here are a few excerpts from some of the reviews:

'Philosophia Botanica is certainly a must on the shelves of anyone interested in the history and philosophy of the life sciences.' Dr Staffan Müller-Wille, *Journal of the History of Biology*, No. 37, 2004

'... reading this excellent translation ... Reviewers of the hard copy edition have already heaped praise on Stephen Freer's skilful and meticulous translation. I can only add gratitude for providing easy

---

* Linnaeus's *Philosophia Botanica*, translated by Stephen Freer. OUP, 2003. Paperback 2005, reprinted 2006, 2007

access to one of Linnaeus's most important texts.' Prof. Pieter Baas, *The Linnean,* October 2006

'Fortunately, Stephen Freer, a classical scholar, has provided a painstaking, exact and very lucid English translation ... so that the *Philosophia Botanica*, with the addition of an excellent introduction by Paul Alan Cox, is now accessible and meaningful to those with no more than a modest grasp of systematic botany.' Desmond Meikle, *Curtis's Botanical Journal,* May 2007

'The translator's meticulous attention to detail and the publisher's lavish production cannot be praised too highly. A valuable resource for taxonomists and of great interest to botanists in general and historians of science.' *The Naturalist,* July 2006

'As translator, Freer is in a sense invisible in this work, and yet his hand is on every page, presenting Linnaeus' ideas and teachings to a new and wider audience ... straightforward and very readable. This translation is an important contribution to science and its history ...' Charlotte Tancin, *Hunt Institute for Botanical Documentation*, June 2006

'Stephen Freer is to be heartily congratulated for providing such a stylish and, for the first time, complete English translation of this most important volume.' Dr Gren Lucas, *Plant Talk,* July 2003

'For his skilful translation, Stephen Freer deserves our unstinted admiration and gratitude.' Philip Oswald, *Archives of Natural History,* October 2004

This peaceful and very happy time in our lives continued. Stephen was spending every day at his desk, a little card index box providing essential details – no computer then – as well as weekly research visits to the Bodleian Library, courtesy of kind neigh-bours Paul and Caroline Weller. (The Wellers' daughter, Atalanta,

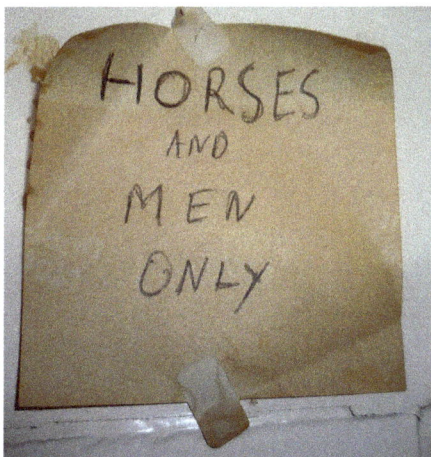

Note that Stephen stuck on study door,
Horses and Men Only

was the same age as Zazie, and they quickly became great friends. I remember, as teenagers, their sneaking cigarettes into the Woodfield kitchen garden, thinking no one could see them, wafts of smoke drifting up over the garden wall. The two eventually shared a house in London and now enjoy spending time together, when possible, with their families.)

The next book was Linnaeus's *Musa Cliffortiana* (Clifford's Banana Plant), commissioned by Professor Tod Stuessy of the IAPT (International Association for Plant Taxonomy) and published in 2007.* This was somewhat lighter, less encyclopaedic and actually a very charming story. (I wrote a children's book about it, *The Banana Party*, as yet unpublished.) Linnaeus, working in the garden of a rich Anglo-Dutchman, George Clifford, in Holland, wanted to see if he could grow a banana tree from seed (in this case from India) as they did in hot countries. Very few in Europe had ever done this before. The Linnean Society photocopied Linnaeus's Latin notes and diaries, and I remember so clearly going into Stephen's study and noticing in the papers on his desk that Linnaeus had reached 24 January 1736, where he had written in Latin in just a few words that the plant had flowered. His experiment had worked. I rushed to tell Stephen, who was having his regular bread and jam and cup of tea at five o'clock in the kitchen and who remained completely unperturbed by the news, focusing on eating, as always.

Throughout the Linnaeus translations, we were fortunate to have the support and help of the great Linnaeus expert Dr Staffan Müller-Wille, who kindly wrote an Introduction to *Musa*, and who would often come to stay with us and who remains a good friend.

Linnaeus became part of our lives. The Linnean Society had kindly given a splendid book launch for *Musa* early in 2007, and in May of that year, the tercentenary of Linnaeus's birth, I read of Swedish royalty coming to London to celebrate at the Society. Stephen and I celebrated rather more quietly with a glass of wine in our kitchen garden, together with our dear neighbour, Julian Leeds.

Stephen, now eighty-seven, said he'd love to work on yet another book. And, so, a fourth came along, *The History of Rarer Plants* (1601) by

---

* Linnaeus's *Musa Cliffortiana*, translated by Stephen Freer. IAPT, 2007

Clusius (Charles de l'Écluse), the French botanist (1526–1609), who was responsible for introducing the tulip from China to the Netherlands, transforming gardens there and throughout Europe ('The father of all the beautiful gardens in Europe'), developing new cultivated plants, such as the potato and the chestnut, from other parts of the world. Clusius spent his later years teaching in Leiden, where his cultivation of tulips in the botanic garden was the beginning of the Dutch tulip bulb industry.

This translation, which Stephen intended to dedicate to our daughter, Zazie, was commissioned by the Royal Botanic Gardens of Madrid. A Spanish professor, Dr Luis Laca, had heard of Stephen from the botanist Professor David Mabberley, as well as from the Linnaean Society. Luis, whose real job was as an architect specialising in historic buildings, came to visit us several times. We so enjoyed introducing him to all our friends, as we had done Staffan Müller-Wille.

We had got about one third through the translation when, alas, Spain ran out of funding and could no longer afford to pay us. Very amusing emails from Luis saying how the chatty bank clerk in the Madrid bank had given him lengthy descriptions of her grandchildren's recent visits before adding, as a mere afterthought, how sorry she was but it wouldn't be possible to forward any payments to Mr Stephen Freer in the UK as Spain had now completely run out of money!

Maybe we should have continued without funding? It was 2013. Stephen was ninety-three. Recently, I was very glad to give Stephen's Clusius translation and papers to Emma Tennant, a great admirer of Clusius and someone I knew would appreciate this small archive and give it a good home.

I wrote and asked Staffan Müller-Wille if he would kindly read the above chapter as I was concerned it might be too long. I also needed to make sure there were no errors. He replied:

I have read the extract you sent from your memoir – charming reading, and really interesting; it felt not too long at all! I was very interested to learn that Stephen managed to translate part of Clusius.

We had had such fun for over twenty-five years, dealing with delightful medical and botanical experts, learned editors and writers ...

Thank you, dear Jane (Brabyn), for introducing us to Dr Christopher Wharton all those years ago.

Stephen (and Boots) beside a copy of Philosophia Botanica
(Wiltshire & Gloucestershire Standard, *2003). Stephen was to tell me later how worried he had been that Pamela Jackson's copy of Nabokov's shocking novel,* Lolita, *on the shelf behind him, might show in the photograph*

Chapter 11

Holidays

There were many but these few stand out in my memory:

The Ile de Ré. Lake Orta. Prague. Seville. Lia. Delphi. Corfu (The British Cemetery in *The Orchid Review*). Wales.

The Ile de Ré, France: I am sure that one of the reasons Stephen married me was because I was half-French. He adored the French and France.

My French mother had a holiday house on the Ile de Ré, an island off the west coast of France, on the Atlantic, opposite La Rochelle. It was full of enchanting, colourful little harbour villages, sailing boats, a splendid bird sanctuary (the brainwave of a British woman, of course, Margaret Critchley). My grandparents, living in Paris, had been caught there during WWII and stayed on till they died. Now horribly fashionable, especially for sailing, it was very primitive indeed in the late 1940s and 1950s when my sister and I would go each year with my mother to stay with her parents.

When I first took Stephen there in 1981, when Zazie was two, it was already buzzing with tourists during the summer. We hired bicycles, like everyone else, and rode to the beach every day. My bike had a special seat at the back for Zazie. We'd take a picnic lunch. I never learnt to swim but Stephen could, after a fashion.

One problem was that the beach we loved most – La Mer Sauvage – on the Atlantic, with very wild high tides and endless sand dunes was, also, though very discreetly, a nudists' beach. We really hadn't taken that in because it was usually very hot and most people, anyway, weren't wearing many clothes.

However, when we arrived and had settled down in our chosen picnic spot on the beach, Stephen would start taking off his clothes. This was quite a slow process, especially as he was usually wearing so many different layers, not having noticed he was now in a fairly hot country: vest, shirt, woolly, jacket, tie, fob watch . . . trousers, socks, leather shoes . . . all had to be removed and safely stored.

By the time he reached his vest, a very discreet but discernible group of Frenchmen and women would have gathered, watching in amusement and surprise. I found this very embarrassing but Stephen didn't notice. Wearing his swimming trunks, he would then very slowly walk into the Atlantic, with its giant waves, do about three very careful strokes and then say, 'I think that's enough.'

This huge white body would then lift itself out of the Atlantic and slowly come back to his pile of clothes . . . and wife and child. After a good drying-down with a towel, all those layers had to be put back on again which, of course, took ages and attracted another small crowd.

The serious business of going to the marché, *shopping list in* French, *Zazie in a pushchair ...*

The daily market in Les Portes, our village on the Ile de Ré – and the last village at the very end of the island – was awesome: enticing stalls full of freshly caught fish, cheese, vegetables, herbs freely offered with whatever you bought. We'd head off there; Stephen dressed as usual, clutching a basket and the shopping list (in French) on this important mission, Zazie in a pushchair.

We spent all our summer holidays on the Ile de Ré until my mother died in 1995.

Lake Orta, Italy: Casa Forbes had been bought in 1927 by my Scottish ancestor, Colonel Lachlan Forbes, son of General Sir John Forbes, who had married Emily Drummond of Megginch Castle, where they then lived. Uncle Lachie left the Casa to my great-uncle, Ernan Forbes Dennis, who, in turn, in 1954, left it to my father, Nigel Dennis. Nigel was now the third generation to own that Italian house, which he loved above all others. (Nigel was to leave the Casa to me in his will. He died in 1989.)

Casa Forbes on Lake Orta showing neighbour's beautiful walled garden hiding our rather smaller one

The Casa was a narrow lakeside four-storey eighteenth-century house in the medieval village of Orta San Giulio on one of the smallest Italian lakes, Lake Orta, set in the foothills of the Alps. There was a pretty narrow garden, with a lawn surrounded by shrubs, and steps going down into the lake – and a little rowing boat. It faced an island on which was a beautiful old monastery that one couldn't help glimpsing throughout the day, enchanted, as the sun moved slowly around it, the colours of the monastery and the lake water changing as it did so.

It was 1985 and Nigel, living with Beatrice in Malta, had never met Stephen or Zazie, now aged six. We knew that Nigel was going to be in Orta for much of the summer and decided to go with Zazie to see him, staying in the Hotel San Rocco on the lake beside Casa Forbes.

It was a very happy visit and we were so glad that we had gone. We enjoyed exploring the old town; the shady, narrow cobbled streets; the faded, peeling paint of the houses; sitting on the Piazza beside the lake, eating ice creams ... On our last day, we invited Nigel to dine with us at the hotel, having drinks first in the gardens. It was all a great joy.

Zazie, aged six, running to greet her grandfather for the first time

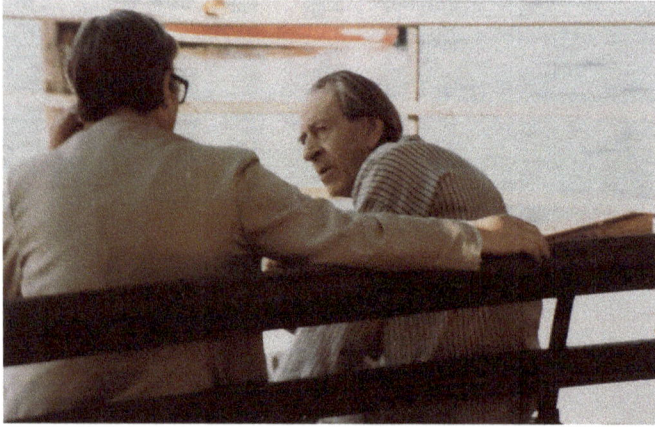

Stephen talking to Nigel by the lake

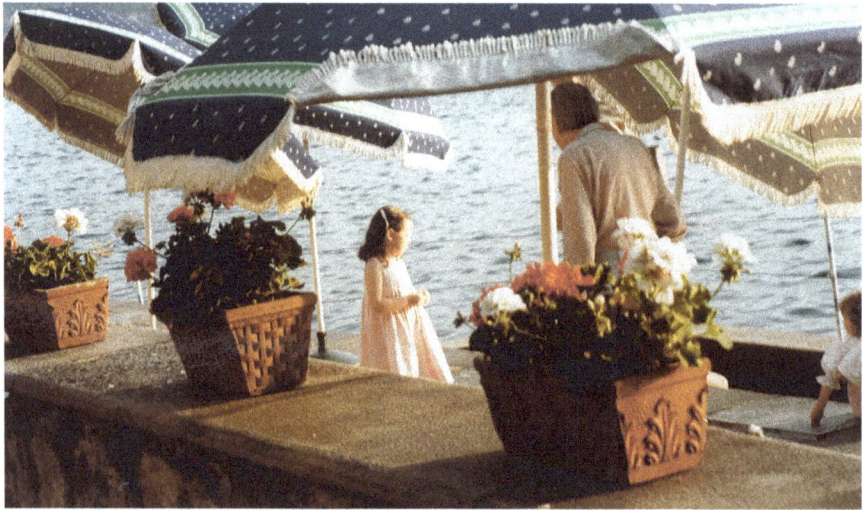

Nigel and Zazie

Prague, Czech Republic: In 1997, Stephen, Zazie and I had a glorious three-day trip to Prague with Jane Brabyn and her daughter, Lowdy, a dear friend of Zazie. Had such fun, Jane and I laughing most of the time whilst exploring all the usual tourist bits, as well as discovering some of our own.

I loved the idea of being in *Bohemia*. I remember a slightly seedy writers' sort of café we particularly liked, with armchairs/sofas, every-one smoking and delicious hot chocolate served with rum. There, a band of rather sozzled grey-bearded anguished musicians would troop in and play for us.

Prague, so beautiful: the river, the castle standing above it, as it does, the cobbled streets, enchanting coloured houses, the city magically lit up by old lights at night, bookshops, like Charing Cross Road . . .

It was on that Prague visit, all of us walking along the Charles Bridge one afternoon, that Jane asked Stephen, 'How's the book going?' (This was Linnaeus's *Philosophia Botanica*.)

Stephen replied, 'Well, I've reached the chapter where Linnaeus talks about the sex lives of plants.'

Zazie and Lowdy, both teenagers, looked absolutely appalled and began to walk very fast indeed, trying hard to distance themselves from these three extraordinary grown-ups talking about sex and plants, especially as Stephen had enthusiastically begun to elaborate on that specific chapter.

Seville (Orange marmalade!), Spain: We had been to many countries but, other than magical holidays in Ibiza with my generous and exceptional Aunt Eve and her husband, David (Henley-Welch), mainland Spain had somehow eluded us. A whole new discovery, Seville becoming quite my favourite city in the world. Stephen and I were invited there in 2003 by dear Jane Brabyn, yet again, when all the orange trees were laden, ripened fruit plopping down onto the ground as you walked along. I had never seen an orange tree before and was enchanted.

The hotel (Las Casas de la Juderia) was made up of a series of elegant old townhouses with several inner fountained courtyards painted mustards and deep blues, a man playing the piano in the evenings, newspapers on sticks . . .

The Seville architecture, a fusion of Christian and Muslim styles, a magnificent cathedral, endless gardens, hidden courtyards lined with the brightest-coloured tiles, tiny narrow cobbled streets with high walls, a splendid palace, Flamenco dancing – Stephen amazed – carriages and horses, endless restaurants in beautiful old houses . . . and an unforgettable day spent in Granada, exploring the Alhambra.

Wherever we went, the Spaniards were unfailingly helpful and beautifully mannered. At last, I understood why Spain is so popular ...

Lia, Greece: We were so privileged to have many holidays in Greece with Nick and Joan Gage. Joan and I had shared an apartment in New York in the 1960s and had remained good friends ever since. Meanwhile, Nick had written a hugely successful book, *Eleni*, about his mother's execution in 1948 in the Greek northern mountains where his family had lived. Nick was eight years old. *Eleni* was made into a film, just as successful as the book. (President Kennedy was a great fan.) More books followed; the one I particularly like, *A Place for Us*, describes the family moving to Boston soon after his mother's death and how they survived, having nothing, selling vegetables on the sidewalk, Nick eventually becoming a journalist for the *New York Times.*

During our holidays, Stephen, Zazie, Polly and I would be based in Nick's mountain village of Lia, in northern Greece, near the Albanian border – now with a hotel, a helipad and a museum, which building

Joan Gage when Zazie and I visited her and Nick in Boston, USA

work had been overseen by Nick's eldest daughter, Eleni, who took a year out from her job in New York to write a book about the restoration of their family house – *North of Ithaca* – which British book launch I had great fun arranging in London.

From Lia, we would travel all over Greece, often in a taxi(!), Joan determined to show us all she could, to share this beautiful country she had got to know so well. I could never believe that Stephen, a classical scholar, had never been to Greece. He was sixty-one. (Something that Joan remembers with affection was Stephen's well-meaning effort to communicate, however briefly – in a shop or to a waiter – in Greek only, of course, it was *ancient* Greek which, unintentionally, caused great amusement and bafflement. After the first day, Stephen realised that no one understood and from then made heroic efforts at short sentences in *modern* Greek, but these were not too successful, either.)

How forever grateful we were for our visits to the Gages', enjoying our last day in Lia which entailed a Greek Orthodox Easter Day service lasting many hours, the congregation quietly coming and going, the endless lighting of candles, the wild asparagus freshly picked up in the hills by a kind elderly man just a few hours before the superb Easter lunch we were to enjoy, in the spring sunshine, cooked and shared with welcoming neighbours.

Corfu*, *Greece: Corfu was explored on one of those delightful visits. Discovering the British Cemetery, full of wild orchids, was an especial joy. Run by a dear, hugely knowledgeable man called George, whose father, before him, had cared for the cemetery, too.

I have printed out below an article I wrote about George and the cemetery which was published in *The Orchid Review*, an RHS publication. The editor kindly supplied all the actual *orchid* information as, of course, I had absolutely no knowledge whatsoever of orchids – and about which article the Corfu British Vice-Consul, amongst others, was so kind.

THE BRITISH CEMETERY, CORFU

At the end of April 2005, my husband and I were once again the guests of our Greek-American friends, writers Joan and Nick Gage, and their daughter, Eleni, also a writer, on the island of Corfu, en route to celebrate Greek Easter in Epiros.

On our first day, we set out to explore areas outside Corfu old town. Firstly, the Achilleion Palace, followed by Mon Repos (Prince Philip's birthplace), and then the British Cemetery. Its approach did not bode well: on a busy road on the outskirts of the old town, next to the prison, and with many newly built houses opposite, we had no idea what lay in store.

Opening the gate, we were met by the caretaker, George Psaila. George, born in

1927, and a British citizen, is of Maltese origin. (His father was one of many Maltese settlers on the island.) He inherited the job from his father, who worked at the cemetery from 1924–1944. George was born in the small shuttered pink house which stands just inside the cemetery gate. Now seventy-eight, George, with the help of his wife and two children, has cherished and tended these peaceful hidden gardens and graves for over sixty years and eagerly shows them to the international visitors who come daily. The British Ambassador to Athens was leaving as we arrived.

The most astonishing thing that greeted us was the proliferation of tiny wild orchids! There are more than forty species, some with several varieties, and a few hybrids, growing wild between the graves and in the open spaces.

[Here I have printed a list of orchids from George's booklets, plus a large contribution about orchids from the Editor in a box on one of the pages of the article.]

Left in the deliberately long, uncut grass, with just a few necessary paths, the impression was of a highly romantic, slightly dishevelled, scented garden alive not only with wild and exotic flowers but with numerous old terracotta tubs and urns, fascinating worn gravestones, monuments, vast, elaborate civic and military memorials, ornate Victorian vaults, sarcophagi and stone curbs, well covered in moss and lichen. And blossoming at the same time were wisteria, Judas trees (Cercis siliquastrum), broom, spring bulbs and arum lilies, so reminding me of Malta, where they grow wild in the hedgerows. At other times of the year, we learnt that there would be Madonna lilies, roses, philadelphus, lilacs, hyacinths, various cacti, amaryllis, agapanthus, anemones, cyclamens, irises and much more, blooming beneath the jacarandas, and the beautiful and rare Californian sequoias.

The orchids begin flowering at the end of February, starting with Barlia robertiana, and finish at the beginning of June with Anacamptis pyramidalis v. brachystachys.

As well as being known for its wild orchids, the cemetery is of great historical interest. It was opened in 1814 during the British Protection of the Ionian Islands. Since then, English soldiers, officers and members of their families have been buried there, as well as many sailors. On the left are the older graves; in the centre there is a large common grave (an ossuary). A memorial stone gives the names of the soldiers who died or drowned in Corfu and Zante and in the trenches of Crimea during the Crimean War (1851–1856). Many soldiers of the 1st and 2nd World Wars are buried there, as well as twelve young sailors of the two British Naval vessels that hit mines on 23 October 1946 in the channel between Corfu and Albania. (Thirty-two more bodies were not recovered.) During the German occupation (1943–1944), fifty-three German soldiers were temporarily buried in the right wing of the cemetery, and there still remain some German graves from the crew of Kaiser's private ships (1890–1910), as well as some recent German graves, because there is no German cemetery in Corfu. Nowadays, English families who live in Corfu also choose the cemetery as their burial place. In all, the total of old and new graves, decorated by the wild flowers, has now risen to over 550.

It can be seen from the Visitors' Book that more than 500 people visit this cemetery every month during the tourist season, amongst them many archaeologists, botanists.

Each year in November, on Remembrance Sunday, a memorial service is held at the cemetery, organised by the British Consulate and the British colony of Corfu.

George's devotion to the graves, and his pride in this impressive collection of wild orchids, was immensely touching. With great agility for his age, he knelt and parted the grasses to point out especially rare and beautiful specimens. Delighted by our interest, he showed us his own headstone, inscribed simply GEORGE! We found that he had written two small illustrated booklets on the cemetery and the orchids, both for sale to visitors. The second book, The Foreigners' Garden, written in 1994, contains colour photographs of the many species of wild orchids found in the cemetery, and begins with George's belief: 'If all people loved flowers, we would never have wars.'

I vowed to see that this modest man receive some recognition for such devotion and then read in the booklets that this had already been done: in 1977, the Commonwealth War Graves Commission awarded George a certificate which read 'Presented by the Commonwealth War Graves Commission in recognition of long and devoted service'. And, in 1988, the Queen, on the recommendation of the British Embassy, awarded George a British Empire Medal 'in recognition of his faithful and conscientious service'.

Surrounded by immensely tall cypresses, away from the bustle of the town, this enchanting oasis was a highlight of a fascinating eight-day trip to Greece. The cemetery is open daily. Entry is free. There are numerous green benches on which visitors can sit and reflect, and a charming, friendly ginger cat, that will join you.

Do not be put off by the busy road alongside the cemetery; our taxi driver did not know where it was but, on mentioning the prison, the problem was instantly solved. (George remembers the hill views from his pink house, before the new houses were built.) Once inside the cemetery gate, none of this matters. You are enclosed in a cherished space, in the privileged presence of a dear, humble man, whose lifetime work is evident all around you.

The Orchard Review, RHS, January 2006

Delphi, Greece: *The following year, we went with the Gages to Delphi, where I can remember one occasion so clearly: Stephen, Nick and I, sitting at the top of a mountain, a dear old lady clapping her hands at some straying goats, reminiscing with Nick about New York where he, Joan and I had lived all those years ago.*

'The thing about New York,' I said, 'is that you really feel you are in the centre of the world. You feel so sorry for anyone in Paris, London, Rome ... or anywhere else.'

'How can you say that,' said Stephen, astonished, 'when we're sitting in *Delphi*?' (How was I to know that Delphi, to classical scholars, is considered the centre of the world?)

Angers, France: Stephen's favourite place in France was Angers. He said throughout our married life, 'I wish I could take you to Angers.'

I didn't really want to go to Angers. In my ignorance, and looking on the map, it was just a huge cathedral town in the middle of France; nothing about it attracted me, which was, of course, entirely my loss. I wish I could say sorry to Stephen right now.

Aberdyfi, Wales: And it was the same with Wales, although Stephen had taken Zazie there when she was very little.

'I'd so love to take you to Wales,' he'd say to me.

But I didn't want to go to Wales, either. I imagined lots of sheep covering endless acres of hills/fields. I liked cities/bright lights/restaurants/taxis ...

But ... one day ... a good friend and neighbour, Penny Wright Neubauer, generously told us about a cottage in Aberdyfi that she'd inherited. ('Freddie: You *have* to spell it Aberdyfi, *not* Aberdovey.')

'Aberdyfi is where we used to go every year for our camping holiday,' said Stephen, his eyes lighting up.

The start of the convoy of the Freer family embarking on their annual drive from Gloucestershire to Aberdyfi for their camping holiday, c. 1925

Stephen with his brothers, reading in tent c. 1930

Stephen, ninety, triumphant, with Penny Wright and son, Will Neubauer, having at last found the exact *spot in the fields where the Freers used to set up their campsite each year*

And so we were invited . . .

This was 2010. Stephen was ninety. It was a most magical holiday; we stayed in a charming bed and breakfast on the harbour, the sun shone every day and, above all, Stephen was able to show Penny, her son, Will, and me *exactly* where the Freer family always set out their camping site. This entailed traipsing over endless uneven muddy fields till, a miracle, Stephen thought we had found the precise spot. We gazed at this bit of overgrown field in awe . . . This was where the Freers had driven very slowly all the way from Gloucestershire each year in order to have this holiday, cooking on campfires, which, Stephen explained, was where he learnt to cook and why he always made so much mess in the kitchen: because he thought he was outside. And where, each year, they met their friends, the Kettles, who lived in a large house in the village and in whose fields the Freers camped, and who so kindly fed and watered them, as necessary.

Each Sunday, the family would walk from their campsite to the local church, having spent ages cleaning their shoes: three tall, thin boys, a tall military father and a formidable mother. (The shoe-cleaning was very important, I understand, as was the setting-up of the tents – who did what. Only Tom and the father were allowed to do this as it required such mathematical skill. I don't remember exactly what Stephen's role was; something sort of very secondary, if he even had a role, though he longed to be helpful.)

Those family camping holidays in Wales were the highlight of Stephen's childhood; no one to cook or clean for them, they were free as air . . .

Our visit to Aberdyfi all those years later was everything Stephen hoped it would be. I could see on the train how excited he was the nearer we got to the station. And it transformed my imagined picture of Wales as just endless rainy fields of sheep into a country of pretty, small, colourful harbours and sunshine. Thank you, Penny.

Chapter 12

A Severe Nervous Breakdown

In 2012, Stephen had a heart attack, which we hadn't actually noticed – he was breathing badly so we went to see our splendid doctor, Stuart Drysdale, who noticed Stephen's swollen legs and ankles. We were sent immediately to the Accident & Emergency Department at Cheltenham Hospital, where Stephen was kept in for several days.

But the heart attack made Stephen very fearful that death was near. This fear turned into terrifying dreams and nightmares about Hell – nothing else came into his tormented mind, day or night.* He just sat in his chair, dozing, thinking how wicked he had been, how useless his life, how terrified he was of death ... No one could persuade him otherwise, although Andrew Bowden, as well as Jeremy Francis and Charles Keen, visiting him frequently, tried hard to do so, as did other kind and concerned neighbours.

He was being carefully monitored by the excellent community mental health nurse Liz Delahaie, from Weavers Croft in Stroud. We preferred to keep him at home rather than let him go into hospital. Gradually, we saw the darkness lift, and in December 2013, Mrs Delahaie felt that Stephen was now well enough not to need any further visits. It was the medication that, in the end, made a great difference: mirtazapine and quetiapine, and other medication for his heart.

---

* Stephen often used to say, over the years, 'Thinking is bad for the health.' I now understood what he meant.

Last years: Stephen's last four years were, mercifully, years of content-ment. He was at peace – no longer afraid. On the little website that I put together for his Latin books, he wrote, under Hobbies:

History, heraldry, reading, emptying the compost, encouraging a very wild herb garden, and walking the dog, very slowly.

And 'walking the dog', called Boots, after Kipling's charming little *black* terrier (ours being a little *brown* half-Norfolk terrier, completely disobedient, of course), led Stephen frequently to our gardener's wife, dear Gladys Stewart, who lived next door and who, quite unbeknown to me, used to give Stephen – *and* Boots – a slice of cake on every visit! I had never quite understood why Stephen, on some days, would reject his usual bread and jam at five o'clock.

All the same, Stephen did feel somewhat embarrassed to be spending so much time in his armchair, sleeping. He mentioned this to Stuart Drysdale, who said, 'Stephen, at your age you should be dozing *all day* in front of the Aga, like an old Labrador ...' which Stephen found very reassuring.

Frequent happy visits from Zazie, now back in London from Los Angeles, still working in the film world, and from kind friends and neighbours. *The Times'* Saturday Latin crossword had just begun to be published and was quite the greatest fun, as well as wonderfully time-consuming; reading; enjoying our lovely kitchen garden, full of fruit and vegetables, still kept beautifully by Gerald and, now, with the help of dear Julian Leeds, our much-loved, indispensable neighbour.

Stephen, ninety-six, Boots and Murphy Russell going to Gladys' next door for their secret slice of cake

Much enjoying The Times' *Latin crossword (Boots in basket) even though Stephen had told Bletchley Park in his interview in 1941 how much he disliked crosswords. These Latin ones were to prove the greatest fun in Stephen's last few months*

CHAPTER 13

Zazie's Engagement

Zazie had moved to Los Angeles in 2007 to work with a director on a big studio film. What was supposed to be an eight-month stay in California turned into six years and a new and exciting life. Stephen and I were delighted for her. She kept in close touch with us, coming home whenever she could. And I was lucky enough to have an exciting and fascinating trip to visit Zazie in Los Angeles, made possible by our Little Compton special friend, Liz Drury, so kindly coming to take care of Stephen. During this trip, I discovered beautiful Spanish-style houses, with elegant tree-filled gardens, fruit and vegetable markets, stunning sea views from high hills (David Hockney's studio amongst them, as was the famous Hollywood sign), all quite unlike the rather loud and over-glamorous corner I had imagined LA to be. Zazie returned to England in 2014, feeling the pull of family and friends.

With Zazie on her return from Los Angeles

Engagement photo of Zazie and Christy Hawkins, February 2017

Something that was to help Stephen greatly was Zazie's engagement to Christy Hawkins early in 2017. It made me happy, too. A charming, erudite, kind man, Christy was educated at Balliol, Oxford and works as a teacher of English. At his ninety-seventh birthday party in February, Stephen announced their engagement.

Meanwhile, Christy and Zazie were keen to support Projects for All, a charity run by a friend, Katrin McMillan, by doing a walking pilgrimage. It was to be called *A Listening Pilgrimage* and, as Christy explained, 'The primary aim of the journey is a way to learn from individuals and communities about how best to support displaced persons seeking sanctuary in Britain.'

They'd start the walk in March in Dover and finish in Scotland on the Isle of Iona. A journey of 650 miles. They had had tremendous support from all their friends, as they were to have from those they met as they walked.

Zazie and Christy in Kent – setting off on their 650-mile pilgrimage

We had moved Stephen's hospital bed downstairs, beside the Rayburn, which was a great joy to me – we were together, with Boots, from morning till night – and to visiting friends. Our dear retired vet, Mick Ponting, had printed and greatly enlarged a huge map, marking the route of the pilgrimage. This was attached to a hard board and placed at the end of Stephen's bed, where he could see it all day long. That map made all the difference possible to those last weeks, Stephen studying the route religiously every morning, helped by frequent phone calls from Zazie, describing yet more.

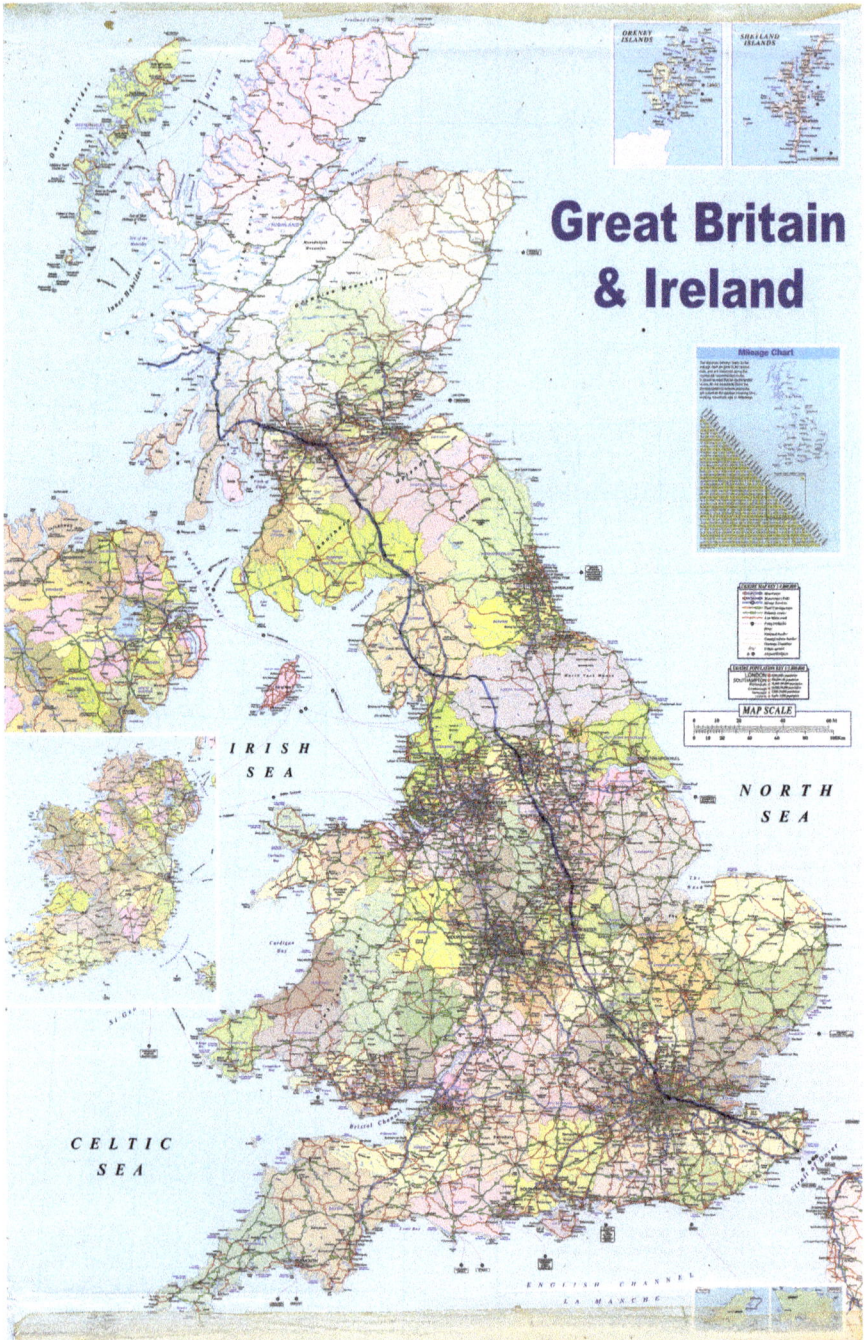

Map of the route, kindly enlarged and marked for Stephen by Mick Ponting

Chapter 14

Stephen's Death and Funeral

Deeply welcome daily supportive visits from kind friends, including Andrew Bowden, Mick Ponting, and Jane Parsons and Penny Wright (both doctors), all of whom were especially good at talking to Stephen, and which visits entailed much laughter and many silly jokes, usually about the dogs or ponies in the old family photographs that I had propped up beside Stephen's bed.

Jane Parsons, Mick Ponting and Penny Wright on one of their many welcome bedside visits, March 2017

It was now early April. Stephen was on End of Life care with excellent help from our local doctor, Clare Henderson, and team at Rendcomb surgery a precious night nurse Rebecca Gamble and three splendid, thoughtful Polish carers from an agency in Tewkesbury called La Vie en Rose, who touched me deeply by coming to pay their respects to Stephen the morning after he died. In no pain or discomfort whatsoever, Stephen's brilliant mind unchanged, our little life continued peacefully.

Zazie temporarily left the pilgrimage in order to spend a few days with us. When she left, two days before Stephen was to die, she said that she'd be back in two weeks. Stephen looked at me and shook his head. He knew … And, a little later, speaking of Zazie's wedding, which was to be in July, Stephen said, 'I'm sorry, darling, but I won't be there.'

Andrew Bowden came yet again the day before Stephen died. He and Stephen talked about our soon-to-be son-in-law, Christy Hawkins, and his new teaching job at Christ's Hospital School in Horsham, which was founded in 1552. Andrew said, 'It must be the oldest educational establishment in the country.'

Stephen said, immediately, 'Oh no, Eton was founded in 1440.'

Andrew and I could only look at each other and laugh. That memory! Undiminished.

The following morning, Stephen said to me, 'Darling, I'm dying.'

A friend, Bev Smith, rang soon after and said, 'Hug him!' which I immediately rushed to do. (I hope I hugged him for the rest of the day.)

Stephen finally stopped breathing at 10pm that evening. It was 26 April 2017. He was ninety-seven years old. It was the most perfect death one could have wished for. No pain whatsoever, warm, loved, at peace … As it said on the death certificate: Frailty of Old Age. I will never cease to be grateful for such an ending.

The funeral at the magnificent medieval Cirencester Parish Church of St. John the Baptist, led by Canon Andrew Bowden, assisted by Rev. Valerie Thorne and Jeremy Francis, and with Zazie and Christy's strong, loving support, was for me, deeply memorable, as was the burial later that same day. This was taken by The Rev. Hugh Williams and

Canon Glyn Evans at the small enchanting Chastleton graveyard where most of the Freer family are buried.

The following three tributes were read out at the funeral:

TOM'S TRIBUTE
Read by Colin Russell

Shortly before he died in 2010, Tom, aged eighty-eight, in Hunter's Nursing Home, asked me to type a tribute to Stephen that he'd just written and that he very much hoped could be read out at Stephen's funeral. Such thoughtfulness was deeply touching. And, of course, the beautiful tribute *was (*most gratefully*)* read out.

I am very lucky to have had Stephen as a brother. I am only two years the younger, and we grew up together, very close.

He said to me in recent years that whenever we were engaged in anything practical, I always took the lead. He may be surprised to know that in all else I took my cue from him, and especially where considerations of moral behaviour came up.

I have remembered for more than eighty years an occasion from our nursery. We had a rather unpleasant nanny, and when Mum finally got rid of her, the replacement was a sweet, gentle girl, from Shropshire. I could be a rather horrible child sometimes, and I started to tease her unmercifully in order to find out what she would do if I went too far. Stephen took me aside and said, 'Stop it! You are not being fair. She is so nice that she will not punish you, so what can she do? Learn how to behave decently!' (Stephen was about six, and I about four.)

Another example when we were at prep school. The Latin master was trans-lating and reading out Caesar. *'Caesar marched into Gaul and conquered them quite easily . . .' The class lapped it up with glee, but Stephen said, 'What business had Caesar to be marching into Gaul? He should have left them alone.'*

Always, you see, Stephen's conscience has been his own; never one to adapt itself to others around him.

He found schoolwork easy, and was a great help to me with Latin grammar,

Greek syntax, and so on. In fact, at the age of about twelve, he wrote for me a Greek Grammar that was far above the official ones provided for our studies; I wish I still had it.

We both found the other boys at prep school rather selfish and quarrelsome. Stephen once told me that the village boys in Little Compton could teach them a thing or two about manners.

Stephen always won any scholarship exam for which he was entered. At one such, when he returned on the evening of the first day, I asked him how it was going. He replied, 'I think it will be all right. I looked round the room at the other candidates when we sat down at the start and they all looked worried.'

At home, we grew up with ponies, then horses. It may surprise you to hear that Stephen was a very good horseman – possibly the best of all of us. Most people see him now as purely academic, but in those days he rode everything easily, like an athlete, although athlete he never was, nor ever wanted to be. I think his secret was a total absence of fear: a horse always senses the rider's feelings, so this is important. Also, a real affection for his horse. We had horses, but were not 'horsey'; ours were part of the family, not objects to be exploited.

He went to Cambridge, winning all the honours all the way. Then came the War. He tried to join the army, but they turned him down on medical grounds; his health had been weakened by several bouts of pneumonia, and in those days there were not the antibiotics we now have.

He was wondering what to do when he was headhunted by Bletchley Park, the famous code-breakers. He was sent for an interview without having the slightest idea what it was about. He was taken on at Bletchley and worked for them for the rest of the War. I don't understand code-breaking, and I always thought it was for mathematicians, not classical scholars. But the people at Bletchley wanted anyone with brains, and Stephen fitted that well.

Bletchley was of course secret. Stephen lodged with a retired engine driver and his wife. Stephen told me they never asked him, when he went to work, what war-work he was engaged in, so he assumed that they knew.

After the War, he joined the Historical Manuscripts Commission in Chancery Lane. His knowledge of languages, and especially of mediaeval Latin, enabled him to translate and catalogue all kinds of documents that came their way. The work was particularly useful to authors needing cross-references about people and periods when they were writing history books. Stephen gained a detailed knowledge of English (and European) history that he has never forgotten; his memory is extraordinary.

Later, he did the same work in the Bodleian Library at Oxford. This was fortunate because when Mum died suddenly, and Dad needed looking after, Stephen could live at home in Little Compton, going from there into Oxford every day. He looked after Dad for seven years, until he died. Stephen has told me that he thinks looking after Dad was the most worthwhile thing he ever did.

Stephen has spent the past twenty years translating (very slowly) four Latin medical and botanical books, two of which have been published by Oxford University Press; one has been described as 'a gift to the world', and another, with the collaboration of the scientific historian Staffan Müller-Wille, who is here today. These translations have given Stephen the greatest pleasure, and Freddie and Zazie enormous pride.

After Dad died, it was not long before he met Freddie; and you know the rest of the story. Marrying Freddie, and the arrival of dear Zazie to complete it, transformed Stephen from a rather solitary soul into a happy family man, and there is nothing better than that. You see, he loves people, but it took some years for that to emerge.

I will conclude with the words that Shakespeare uses at the end of Hamlet:

'Good-night, Sweet Prince.
May flights of angels sing
Thee to thy rest.'

MY COUSIN STEPHEN
by John Budgen (read by John himself)

As one of the dwindling number of Stephen's generation, I trace my conscious recollection of this the most distinguished of us all to the first year of the War when my brother and I were billeted for nine months with Stephen's parents at Oakham – a large house near Little Compton which was the Freer home for a good many years.

Being a member of the Freer family was, you could say, an experience. Stephen's mother was innately very kind but, as her sister, my own mother, always said, she didn't really know how to put it into effect. The most immediate shock was having to have a ritual cold bath every morning. This seemed to me a quite unnecessary precaution against what? I wondered.

Then there was the drawing room where, in the evenings, we would gather. This was a long and lofty room in which burned a rather unsuccessful fire halfway along. Uncle Charlie and Aunt Mina sat close to the fire on either side, and the rest of us made out in the chillier space further out. At the back of this meagre fire was a back-boiler which fed a radiator in the attic where the three boys slept. This was a major concession to decadence but, as they had to put anti-freeze in the system, I doubt that the boys felt that they were spoiled. Some years later, we did the Spartans at school and I had a strange sense that I understood how the term became an adjective.

The boys had a sitting room which was called The School Room.

The cook was Mayes, a genial (to me, ancient) lady who was easily the most homely thing about the place.

The little terrier, Gussie, was a great character and on the way back from church, was put out of the car to run up the hill. He arrived coughing vigorously and Aunt Mina used to say, 'Yes, it's his heart, you see.' I don't know how his heart survived but he was clearly a dog of great perseverance.

My aunt sometimes played the organ at Chastleton church when Mrs Whitmore Jones was away. Mrs Whitmore Jones had a shaking left hand which added to her playing an element of chance. When Aunt Mina was playing, we used to go over for her to practise, and I would blow the organ, which I suppose was my first contact with the instrument which has preoccupied me now for nearly seventy years.

I have spoken a lot about Stephen's parents and less about him, but this is to give you a bit of background to his upbringing.

The three Freer brothers were all at least ten years my senior, and thus a source of mystery and condescension, and I saw little of them until Christmas. I do recall Stephen as a student of the violin, but as music-making was confined to the further reaches of that drawing room, the winter holidays were not the time to hear much of it.

Uncle Charlie was at this time heavily into beekeeping and one day a friend brought over a separator which whirled the honeycombs round at great speed, delivering the honey out of a drain at the bottom. The two men were impressed with the results and thought it would be interesting to see the process at first hand. They took the lid off, covering the entire kitchen in a fine and sticky mist of honey. My aunt ordered Uncle Charlie, the friend and the new toy out of the kitchen, and they were not seen again for some time.

I cannot say that I saw very much of Stephen in the ensuing twenty years. But I do remember well, when Aunt Mina died, how splendidly Stephen rose to the task of looking after his father.

Stephen's marriage was a great delight to all the family, as was the birth of Isabel.

Naturally impressed by his enormous erudition and his instant recall of all that it encompassed, it has always been a pleasure as well as a source of knowledge to see him, giving me cause to regret that I did not always see more of him.

Such are a few recollections of a surviving cousin,
John Budgen

TRIBUTE BY PROFESSOR DR STAFFAN MÜLLER-WILLE
Read by Charles Keen

In memoriam Stephen Freer

Stephen was not a man of many words, as we all know. But he had an inexhaustible curiosity for words and what they mean in different languages. Late in his life, when others are glad to 'retire', Stephen began to publish English translations of early modern works in science, first Thomas Wharton's Adenographia *of 1656, the first European treatise to deal with glands as a separate organ system, and then* Philosophia Botanica, *a book by the Swedish naturalist Carl Linnaeus that taught how to name and classify plants.*

It was through the latter translation, which came out in 2003 with Oxford University Press, that I got to know Stephen. I had published an enthusiastic review of Stephen's translation in the Journal for the History of Biology, *and Freddie got in touch with me with a desperate request for a new translation project to keep Stephen busy. It took several starts, but finally we settled on translating Linnaeus's* Musa Cliffortiana *of 1736, a charming coffee table-like book on the banana which Gunnar Broberg, a professor in Lund, had suggested.*

For two years, I then had the privilege of regular visits to Caudle Green, a little world of its own. I enjoyed beautiful walks and garden visits with Freddie, savoury lunches and dinners with intriguing guests, but above all long morning and afternoon sessions in Stephen's study, crammed with old books, and an ingle always crackling along. Musa Cliffortiana *is a truly baroque work with several layers of puns and metaphors that extol the virtues of Linnaeus's mentor, George Clifford, a Dutch banker of English descent, but also unveil the mysteries of banana reproduction, sometimes in terms we would today think of as too 'explicit' to be scientific.*

I will never forget how Stephen had a merry chuckle to himself whenever he hit on a particularly good solution to convey these layers of meaning in English, or when he had finally worked out what a particularly obscure name of a plant, person or place actually referred to. Words, even in Latin, were not 'dead' for him but teeming with an eternal life of their own. Stephen was a philologist in the true sense of the word, and I am grateful to have had the privilege to share my love for words with him.

Zazie has always felt deeply sad not to have been with us at the end. It was a difficult decision: Stephen, we know, preferred to think of her and Christy on that walk ('A Listening Pilgrimage'). The point of this walk gave him such pleasure. Had she left it for a few weeks – it could have been months – he would have known why she had done so and felt very unhappy about such a decision. As it was, the pilgrimage – and Mick Ponting's huge map showing their route – were the joys of Stephen's last few weeks; knowing that Zazie was with this delightful, kind man, whom she was going to marry, on a walk of which Stephen so approved. This is what Stephen wanted, but I can understand that it was sad for Zazie.

A few months after Stephen's death, I read an article in *The Times* by a doctor, Rachel Clarke, on her father's death. It said all the things I had been feeling; mostly, deep *gratitude*. I was asked to join a local grieving group but explained that I wasn't actually grieving but, rather more, enormously *grateful*; grateful to have had such a husband and grateful that such a dear man of ninety-seven could have had such a peaceful, painless death. (I should certainly not have been at all 'grateful' had the end been painful or, indeed, if Stephen had suffered in any way at all. As it was, I couldn't have asked for more.)

Emma Tennant wrote an obituary for *The Times* and contributed to one for the *Daily Telegraph*. Words cannot describe what those obituaries meant – and still mean – to me. Emma encapsulated everything about Stephen that was precious to Zazie and me; there was nothing I could have added.

I look back on my marriage to Stephen not only as a happy, fulfilled one, albeit with regret at my failings, but rather more as a privilege – a privilege that Zazie shares with me – to have been so close to such a uniquely good, innocent, trusting, supremely modest, gentle and sweet man, his brilliant brain a mere bonus.

Stephen Freer

Classical scholar and Bletchley codebreaker

At the age of 20 Stephen Freer was recruited as a codebreaker at Bletchley Park straight from university in what he described as "a rather unorthodox way". In fact there was nothing orthodox about the assembling of that remarkable group of individuals who worked at Bletchley, and would turn the course of the Second World War.

That Freer was a scholar with a brilliant and original mind may have explained why he stood out, but it was by chance, after he had failed his army medical, that he was brought to the attention of MI6. A friend of an uncle knew the chief personnel officer at the agency and suggested he might be interested in a young man who had won the top scholarship to Eton, and another at Cambridge, where he was reading classics.

At an interview in London in 1940, Freer was told, "in strict confidence" that the job was in naval intelligence and had to do with breaking the enemy's codes and cyphers. Later, he was summoned to an interview in Oxford. He missed his train, had no time to change, and turned up in an old jacket and grey flannel trousers to find himself being questioned by Commander Alastair Denniston, head of the Government Code and Cypher School, and founder of Bletchley Park. Denniston had already brought in brilliant men like Alan Turing, who cracked the German Enigma code.

Denniston asked Freer whether he was "air-minded" — interested in planes — to which he replied, "Not at all," and then if he did crosswords, to which the answer was that he hated them. Far from falling down on these obvious qualifications, he was immediately offered a job by Denniston, who was impressed by his frankness.

Training in London was eventually followed by assignment to Bletchley Park, where Freer worked under Gerry Morgan, the head of the research section, using the Hagelin machine to crack ciphers from the Italian navy, which was supplying the Germans in north Africa. "Every now and then, after we had deciphered a message about a convoy from Naples, a few days later we would read in the paper that a convoy had been bombed on its way to north Africa, and we thought we had achieved something there," he said recently.

Freer also worked with William Tutte, who gained fame as the solver of the "Tunny" cipher, which was used by Hitler to communicate with his generals.

In early 1942 Freer followed Denniston, who had been replaced at Bletchley Park by Edward Travis, to London. The research operation moved to an old hat shop in Berkeley Street, where the hats were still in store, and incoming traffic was received and noted down by

Stephen Freer at Eton

Continued on page 58

CONTINUED FROM PAGE 57
Stephen Freer

two women who had started as telegraph clerks in the reign of Queen Victoria. Freer was attached to the Japanese section, where he found a way of decoding diplomatic messages sent from Germany and Italy, despite knowing no Japanese. The team did so without machines, establishing word patterns, and noting recurring differences that let them decipher messages, which were passed to translators.

Stephen Drake Freer was born at Little Compton, Warwickshire, in 1920. His father, Reginald Charles Freer, was a retired army officer. His mother, Mina Kindersley, was the daughter of an Eton housemaster. Stephen and his two brothers grew up in an intellectual household. His mother insisted that they had cold baths every morning. Stephen became a fearless rider who hunted with the Heythrop hounds.

His love of languages was soon apparent. Aged 12 he wrote a Greek grammar for his younger brother, Tom, which was far better than the one provided by their prep school, Scaitcliffe. In due course he went to Eton, which he enjoyed, and was at Trinity College, Cambridge when war broke out.

The strain of his wartime work exacted a toll on his health, and it took him some time to settle into civilian life. He then found congenial work with the Historical Manuscript Commission, much of it in the libraries and archives of country houses, and in the Bodleian Library, where he worked on medieval manuscripts with two great scholars, Richard Hunt and Bill Hassall.

His extraordinary memory meant that he never forgot a date or a detail discovered during his research. In 1996 the Oxford University Press published his translation of Thomas Wharton's *Adenographia* published in Latin in 1656, which was the first European treatise to describe glands as a separate organ system. This was followed in 2007 by his translation of Linnaeus's *Philosophia Botanica*, and his *Musa Cliffortiana* (1736), which reveals the mysteries of the reproductive system of the banana. These translations gained international interest and led to new friendships with, for instance, Professor Staffan Müller-Wille of the University

Freer's translations of early scientific treatises brought him international attention

of Lübeck, whose tribute was read at Freer's funeral. As the professor pointed out, although Stephen was a man of few words, Latin words were not dead for him, but teemed with eternal life.

In 1974 Freer had married Frederica Dennis, the daughter of the novelist and playwright Nigel Dennis. Their daughter, Isabel, known as Zazie, now works in films. At Freer's 97th birthday party he announced Zazie's engagement to Christy Hawkins, a young intellectual after his own heart.

Although he became frail, Freer's mind remained sharp, and, having overcome his earlier aversion, he enjoyed the *Times* Latin crosswords. A man of deep faith, he was a Church of England lay reader. His sermons will be remembered for their succinct explanations of such theological problems as the Nestorian heresy. He was buried at Chastleton, where his mother once played the organ, and it was more than appropriate that the last journey of a classical scholar should be along the Roman road, the Fosse Way, which leads from Cirencester — the Roman Corinium — towards Chastleton.

Stephen Freer, codebreaker and classical scholar, was born on February 18, 1920. He died on April 26, 2017, aged 97

Stephen's obituary – The Times *2 June 2017*

Stephen Freer

Classical scholar and translator who decoded Italian an<!--truncated-->

STEPHEN FREER, who has died aged 97, was a classical scholar who translated works of natural history from the Latin, having served during the war decoding Italian and Japanese ciphers at Bletchley Park.

He was born on February 18 1920 at Little Compton, Oxfordshire, and educated at Eton and Trinity College, Cambridge, where he was a classical scholar. Having suffered ill health as a child, he was passed unfit for military service on the outbreak of war. Instead, in 1940, he was approached by the chief personnel officer of MI6 who was recruiting for Naval Intelligence, and later summoned to an interview in Oxford to which he turned up in a scruffy old jacket and flannel trousers.

"One of the people who interviewed me was Alastair Denniston [head of the Government Code and Cypher School]," Freer recalled in an interview, "and I was asked whether I was at all air-minded. I said 'Not at all' and I think my frankness rather impressed them. They also asked me whether I did crosswords, and I said no, in fact I really hate them!"

Despite such unpromising beginnings, he was taken on and joined the Bletchley Park research section under Gerry Morgan, working on deciphering Italian Navy messages. Every now and then, he recalled, "after we had deciphered a message about a convoy from Naples, a few days later we would read in the paper that a convoy had been bombed on its way to North Africa, and we thought we had achieved something there."

Portrait of a Scholar: **Stephen Freer in 1944 by Sir Robin Darwin**

One of his colleagues was William Tutte, who became famous as the main solver of the "Tunny" cipher used by Hitler to communicate with his generals. Freer recalled one occasion when a hypothesis on which Tutte had been working for several months turned out to be wrong and his reaction had been "to retire into a corner from which deep sighing was heard."

Japanese ciphers at Bletchley Park

In 1942 the Diplomatic Section at Bletchley was moved to London and Freer found himself working in the premises of an old hat shop in Berkeley Street and, for a spell, out of a flat in Park Lane. At one point he was deciphering codes used by the Free French because there was a fear that the organisation had been infiltrated by fascist agents.

Later he was attached to the Japanese section. He did not speak Japanese – all the codes were in numbers – and once a code had been broken, it would be taken to the translators, most of whom were diplomats or consuls who had served in the East and knew Japanese, but did not know about cryptography. Freer would later confess that the only Japanese words he could recall were "cherry blossom" and "goodbye".

Freer never told his family and friends about what he was doing and later recalled being shocked when, in 1974, FW Winterbotham published *The Ultra Secret* about his time at Bletchley, the first book to reveal details of what went on there.

When the war ended, the pressure of Freer's work during that time took its toll on his mental health, leaving him fragile for a number of years. But he went on to find great satisfaction in his work for the Historical Manuscripts Commission, which involved exploring the archives of some splendid houses. He later did voluntary work in the manuscript department of the Bodleian Library and then on a part-time basis at the Oxfordshire County Records Office.

He was an enthusiastic member of the Heraldry Society and much of his courtship with Frederica Dennis, whom he married in 1974, was conducted in damp, dark churches while he called out the description of a hatchment he was examining in the far reaches of the roof, all in heraldic language – which she had never heard before.

In 1992 Freer was asked by Oxford University Press to translate Thomas Wharton's *Adenographia* (1656), a history of the glands, from Latin into English. This led to his translation of Linnaeus's *Philosophia Botanica* (1751, published in English in 2007) and *Musa Cliffortiana* (1736, published in English in 2007).

In 1988 he was admitted as a lay reader in the Diocese of Oxford and his faith remained at the heart of all he did.

Always something of an eccentric, he never looked out of windows to see if it was sunny or rainy and wore the same clothes whatever the weather. He also never noticed anyone's background or accent; he treated all he met with kindness and respect.

Freer was a fellow of the Linnean Society of London, and in later life, despite expressing a loathing of crosswords in his youth, he enjoyed doing them in Latin. He listed his hobbies as "history, heraldry, reading, emptying the compost, encouraging a very wild herb garden, and walking the dog, very slowly".

He is survived by his wife and their daughter.

Stephen Freer, born February 18 1920, died April 26 2017

Stephen's obituary – the Daily Telegraph *4 May 2017*

Chastleton. Stephen's headstone designed by Judith Verity (The Lettering Arts Trust)